The Butterflies

OF THE WHITE MOUNTAINS
OF NEW HAMPSHIRE

The Butterflies

OF THE WHITE MOUNTAINS OF NEW HAMPSHIRE

Warren J. Kiel

Illustrations by Lois De Luca

AUDUBON SOCIETY
OF NEW HAMPSHIRE

FALCON®

GUILFORD, CONNECTICUT
HELENA, MONTANA

AN IMPRINT OF THE GLOBE PEQUOT PRESS

Falcon and FalconGuide are registered trademarks of the Globe Pequot Press.

Text and cover design by Nancy Freeborn
Map by Stefanie Ward © The Globe Pequot Press

PHOTOGRAPHY CREDITS: Paul Catling: p. 86; Jay Cossey: pp. 48, 66, 110, 112, 142, 146; Laura Deming: p. 44; David Govatski: p. 196, top; Peter Hall: pp. 10, 34, 40, 42, 88, 94, 98, 124, 138, 156, 160, 162; Don Lafontaine: pp. 18, 102; Geoffrey Niswander: pp. 14, 16, 74, 114, 126, 130, 135, 144, 154, 168; Paul A. Opler: pp. 2, 4, 6, 8, 12, 20, 22, 24, 26, 28, 30, 32, 36, 50, 52, 54, 60, 62, 64, 70, 72, 76, 78, 80, 82, 84, 91, 92, 100, 104, 107, 108, 116, 118, 121, 122, 132, 136, 140, 148, 150, 158, 174; Jim Troubridge: pp. 56, 128, 164.

Library of Congress Cataloging-in-Publication Data
Kiel, Warren J.
      The Butterflies of the White Mountains of New Hampshire / Warren J. Kiel ; illustrated by Lois De Luca. — 1st ed.
         p. cm.
      Includes bibliographical references (p.).
      ISBN 0-7627-2690-3
      1. Butterflies—White Mountains (N.H.) I. Title.

QL551.W47K54 2003
595.78'9'097422—dc21

                                      2002041644

Manufactured in the United States of America
First Edition/First Printing

Dedicated to the memory of

Donald J. Lennox and Lionel Paul Grey

Acknowledgments

Heartfelt thanks to Stephen Walker for inspiration, Dave Govatski and Miranda Levin for patience and perseverance, artist Lois De Luca for transforming my mounted specimens into "living gems," and, especially, to countless friends and colleagues of amateur and professional entomology.

Warren Kiel

I am grateful for the help of Stephen Walker, for the specimens supplied by Warren Kiel, and for the reference material and books supplied by the Audubon Society of New Hampshire. I am also deeply grateful for the help and patience of my husband, Ronald.

Lois De Luca

The Audubon Society of New Hampshire wishes to acknowledge the Mt. Washington Auto Road for its assistance with photography.

Contents

Foreword

Warren J. Kiel, of Whitefield, New Hampshire, epitomizes the concept of a paraprofessional—a so-called "amateur"—whose knowledge in a field outside his occupation equals, or exceeds, that of many trained professionals. Warren works as a skilled craftsman of fine furniture. His avocation involves a lifelong study of lepidoptera: moths, butterflies, and skippers, his personal passion and area of professional expertise.

Warren spent most of his early childhood in the Pompano Beach region of southern Florida, where he graduated from Pompano Beach High School in 1960 and then spent two years studying forestry and biology at the Lake City Ranger School and the University of Florida. He began observing lepidoptera in his early teens and started a professional-quality collection at the age of fifteen. During his youth he spent his summers in northern New Hampshire. His father worked as auditor at the old Waumbek Hotel in Jefferson. There Warren met a local florist and naturalist named Don Lennox, who had an immense impact on him. Warren and Don spent many summers hiking the White Mountains of northern New Hampshire, with Don honing and developing Warren's interests in local natural history. In addition Don spent several winters at Pompano Beach, where he and Warren also studied the local lepidoptera. To this day Warren employs Don's unique and extremely efficient curating techniques.

Warren Kiel is the generally acknowledged local expert on the lepidoptera of northern New Hampshire, especially the White Mountain region. Over a period of some thirty years of residence in Coos County, he has compiled a singular, highly selective, and meticulously curated collection of lepidoptera, mostly from New Hampshire. An unofficial recognition of his brilliant work is reflected by the numerous professional lepidopterists who have visited him at Whitefield or borrowed specimens to compile major monographs on the lepidoptera of the region. The list of visitors to Warren's humble abode would read like a "who's who" of North American professional lepidopterists; also many amateurs peregrinate to Whitefield to secure advice on the local fauna. Whitefield has become an epicenter of knowledge for many persons with serious interests in the lepidoptera of the greater White Mountain region.

His collection and meticulously kept records, compiled over a long period of time, are indeed scientific treasures that will, with the onslaught of development and the destruction of many unique habitats, become priceless. They are an irreplaceable record of the lepidopteran fauna of the region. Most remarkably, all of Warren's work has been entirely supported by personal funds. Furthermore, I've never known anyone, much less one working in science, to accomplish so much with so little equipment. Only recently did Warren receive a gift of a secondhand binocular microscope.

Warren's interest in lepidoptera has run the intellectual taxonomic gamut from butterflies to the larger and more conspicuous "macro" moths to the extremely challenging and relatively unknown group of many families of moths known as the "micros." He has recently collaborated with Dr. Dave Wagner (University of Connecticut) in working with these latter families. He is an expert on the nuances of local variation in structure within a species and on local distribution patterns. He has always freely and most cheerfully given his time and expertise to all who have asked. My students have often been awed and immeasurably rewarded by his knowledge, curatorial skills, humor, and sense of professionalism. In these days of multifarious threats to the local biodiversity of any region and professional self-interest, his work shines as an extraordinary individual achievement in that he has illuminated, and continues to illuminate, all of us about the lepidoptera of one small region.

I know of no other person better qualified to write about the general taxonomy and life history of the butterflies and skippers of the White Mountains of New Hampshire. Surely, those who use this book will be stimulated to make their own contributions to our knowledge of this extremely important group of insects. Warren's work stands as an exemplary model of what one paraprofessional can accomplish. Would that there were many more like him!

Donald H. Miller, Ph.D.
Professor of Biology, Department of Science
Lyndon State College, Lyndonville, Vermont

Preface

In the pursuit of one's avocation, be it butterflies, ancient tombs, or any other mystery, serendipity sometimes prevails. Serendipity played a large role in the creation of this book. It all began on a clear and warm July morning in 1995, when Dave Govatski, manager of the Audubon Society of New Hampshire's Pondicherry Wildlife Refuge, and I set out for a canoe and kayak excursion. Our objective was to see as much of the dead water of Little Cherry Pond as possible. It was a rewarding day in an extraordinary place with the usual suspects making appearances, including a bull moose feeding on cow lilies at the pond's edge in all its velvety splendor and a new orchid for the plant list. On the trip out, however, along a sweltering section of abandoned railroad bed, we made our greatest find.

To the uninitiated, the appearance of this figure might have evoked images from *One Flew over the Cuckoo's Nest*. To this naturalist, however, its movements appeared every bit as practiced, poised, choreographed, and athletic as those of an Olympic-caliber rhythmic gymnast. A closer inspection of the dancing figure revealed a smallish, white-haired, bearded man, dressed from head to toe in khaki. The tool of his trade, a gossamer white net, was seemingly as large as himself. Dave and I wanted to meet this man because of our interest in everything wild relating to one of the Audubon Society of New Hampshire's most treasured natural areas, the Pondicherry Refuge. A conversation ensued. Warren (for it was Warren Kiel) shared his love of insects with us and promised to send us a list of the species he had identified in the area.

Warren was indeed a rare find. Many months later, and as unexpectedly as our first encounter, a package arrived on my desk. Instead of a simple list as expected, the work was quite a bit more detailed.

Several hundred miles to the south and west in the abandoned farmlands of the Delaware River Valley, Lois De Luca, my mother-in-law, had begun to catalogue the flowers dotting the landscape around her home in Hancock, New York, by painting them. Her keen interest in all things natural included butterflies. Having raised several, she had already begun field sketches of a few of the more common species on their host plants. When she showed me these works, the idea of illustrating Warren's work was launched.

Back in Hillsboro, New Hampshire, I placed a call to my friend and neighbor Annette Cottrell (1907–1997). Annette was an ardent conservationist who had written an article entitled "Observations on New Hampshire Butterflies" for the July 1967 issue of the *New Hampshire Audubon Quarterly*. We had had several conversations over the years regarding butterflies, and she had always felt that not enough was being done on their behalf. In her eyes nothing could be more important than the conservation of a little-known and little-understood group of creatures. Annette generously provided the seed money and her valued experience to get the project going.

Much later I learned of one other relationship. Annette spoke of one of her early experiences with butterflies, one which helped to captivate her lifelong interest. It was a trip to the summit of Mount Katahdin, in Maine, with Don Lennox to search for the Katahdin Arctic. As you will read, 100 miles to the southwest, the very same Don Lennox sparked a lifelong interest in a young Warren Kiel.

Serendipity! By this point the idea had truly metamorphosed. Under the able direction of Miranda Levin, Communications Director for the Audubon Society of New Hampshire, a last and final pursuit began, the making of a book. With the able work of Dave Govatski, support for this project among other conservationists grew. What began as a chance discovery was well on its way to becoming something nobody could have ever imagined would be created. What has emerged, you will find, is part field guide, part naturalist's journal, and wholly a work that will contribute immensely to the conservation of butterflies. I hope that this book will enchant the millions of visitors to this unique region of New England, students of conservation, backyard naturalists, and lovers of natural history illustration alike.

Stephen Walker, Executive Director
Silk Farm Audubon Center
Concord, New Hampshire

AREA MAP

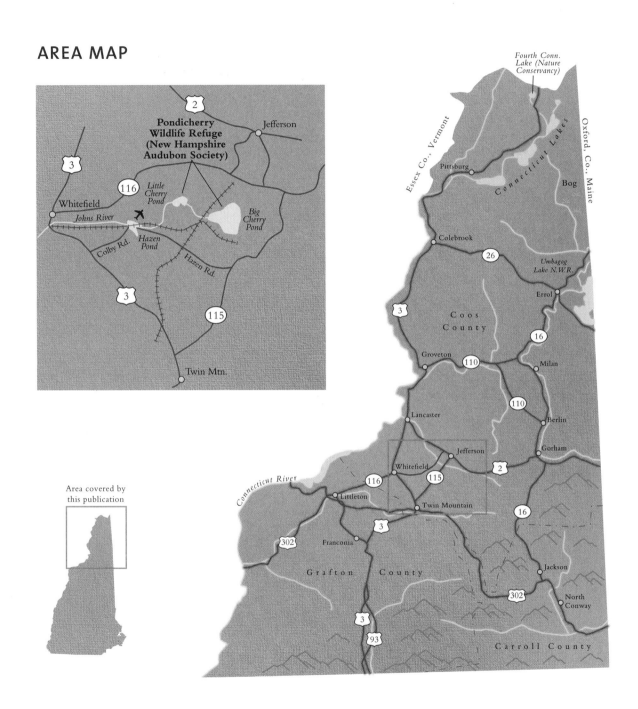

Fourth Conn. Lake (Nature Conservancy)

Pondicherry Wildlife Refuge (New Hampshire Audubon Society)

Jefferson

Whitefield

Johns River

Little Cherry Pond

Big Cherry Pond

Colby Rd.

Hazen Pond

Hazen Rd.

Twin Mtn.

Essex Co., Vermont

Pittsburg

Connecticut Lakes

Oxford, Co., Maine

Bog

Colebrook

Umbagog Lake N.W.R.

Errol

Coos County

Milan

Groveton

Berlin

Lancaster

Gorham

Area covered by this publication

Jefferson

Whitefield

Connecticut River

Littleton

Twin Mountain

Franconia

Grafton County

Jackson

North Conway

Carroll County

Introduction

A Little History

My interest in natural history began at around age ten, during the early 1950s, when I first became fascinated with birds and, later, insects, plants, and flowers. My summers were spent in Jefferson, where my father was employed at the Waumbek Hotel. There I met Donald J. Lennox, hotel florist, who provided answers to my endless questions about these subjects. Donald was a well-known local naturalist with an extensive knowledge of the White Mountain region and, as I quickly learned, a personal collection of butterflies and moths at his home in the Jefferson Meadows. Donald and his delightful wife, Vivian Lennox, invited my parents and me to their home for dinner one evening, and, after the formalities, Donald brought out a number of specimen cases. I was awestruck to see just a portion of his magnificent collection. At that point my young life became changed forever: This was something that I had to learn to do. In the months and years to follow, Donald taught me the basics of curating and observation and collecting techniques and introduced me to the wide array of local habitats. We later did much of our work together, and I accompanied him on countless field excursions, learning new things each time.

Donald grew up in Jefferson and, as a self-taught naturalist, was an endless source of information on plants, birds, and the world of insects; he was also an expert gardener. His own interest in lepidoptera began in the late 1920s, when he formed a local collection and later corresponded and exchanged specimens with amateur and professional collectors throughout North America, including Charles Remington, Douglas C. Ferguson, and well-known entomologist Paul Ehrlich. Remington and Ferguson were frequent visitors and accompanied Donald on many local collecting trips. Through this process of accommodating specialists and sharing information and specimens, much new knowledge was gained about our local fauna, and collected material from here has been added to major museums in the United States and Canada. Several recent definitive works on moths contain plate figures of specimens from Donald's collection, and, over the years, several new specimens have been described. Donald's vast knowledge of plants enabled him to focus much of his attention on lepidoptera early stages, and he was successful in rearing a huge number of species to determine their host-plant affinities. I was fortunate to have Donald to teach me this, as it is all too often neglected by many present-day "specimen" hunters.

Donald spent a number of winters in Florida, working at our companion resort hotel, so his collection expanded to include much southeastern material. His exchanges with collectors from many states added to his collection interesting and unusual species from the Rocky Mountains, desert regions, and Pacific Coast. In the late 1960s Donald worked closely with several entomologists from the University of New Hampshire, participating in light-trap-survey work. Donald donated his huge collection of more than 15,000 specimens to the University of New Hampshire shortly after the death of his wife in 1970. His species card index was later entrusted to me, and I use it constantly in my own continuing work on our lepidoptera fauna. Moreover, his important collection, especially rich in local species, will continue to expand our knowledge as it is accessed by students and specialists for many years to come.

Some Notes on Amateur Collecting

Amateur, or avocational, insect collecting has been popular with many people since Victorian times, when the post-Darwinian era gave rise to huge numbers of enthusiastic observers and field collectors of natural history who enjoyed combining scientific inquiry with the thrill of the hunt and the thirst for adventure. Probably originating in pre-Victorian Europe, this popular hobby infiltrated every social and economic stratum and age level, quickly spilling over into the New World. In North America the precarious avenues westward offered to frontiersmen and scholars alike the natural richness and diversity of a new continent. Insect collecting, along with the collection of new bird, mammal, and plant species, soon enriched our public natural-history institutions and formed the basis for our modern concepts of biodiversity. Insects, because of their relative ease of capture, great variety of form and structure, and uncomplicated prepara-

BUTTERFLY CLASSIFICATION
Order: Lepidoptera

Papilionoidea: True Butterflies

1. SWALLOWTAILS: *Family Papilionidae*

2. WHITES AND SULPHURS: *Family Pieridae*

3. BLUES, COPPERS, AND HAIRSTREAKS: *Family Lycaenidae*

4. BRUSH-FOOTED BUTTERFLIES: *Family Nymphalidae*

5. SATYRS AND WOOD NYMPHS: *Family Nymphalidae (Subfamily Satyridae)*

6. THE MONARCHS: *Family Nymphalidae (Subfamily Danaidae)*

Hesperioidea: Skippers

7. SKIPPERS: *Family Hesperiidae*

1. Canadian Tiger Swallowtail
2. Orange Sulphur
3. Spring Azure
4. Eastern Comma
5. Northern Pearly Eye
6. Monarch
7. Silver-spotted Skipper

tion for exhibit, quickly became a popular hobby with scores of nonprofessional naturalists, and the inherent beauty of butterflies and moths attracted many enthusiastic collectors to this specific order: the Lepidoptera.

Amateur "bug hunters" have historically been a curious lot, often attracting the amused attention of the uninitiated and becoming popularized in fiction, poetry, and Hollywood movies. Collectors are usually portrayed as "absent-minded professors," wildly running across a field while waving an insect net. In his early reference works on butterflies and moths of North America, W. J. Holland frequently refers to the interesting and often humorous escapades of collectors, whose personality types, which range from eccentric to obsessive, often exemplify the avocation of amateur entomology. The humorous little poem "Uncle Jotham's Boarder" by Annie T. Slosson (1838–1926) typifies the way many amateur collectors are perceived: with suspicion, scorn, or, at least, a wary curiosity:

> He'd see a poor miller a-flyin' along,—
>   The commonest, every-day kind,—
> And he'd waddle on arter it, fat as he was,
>   And foller up softly behind,
> Till he'd flop that-air bait-net right over its head,
>   And I'd laugh till nigh out of my mind.

Popular mythology, however, often leads to unfair stereotyping, or, at best, a misleading impression by the casual observer. However amateur entomologists are presented in books, movies, or the press, the demeanor of their real-life counterparts is most often quite different from the way they are frequently portrayed, and their value and contributions to the science of entomology usually understated. Perhaps, then, I can try to correct some of these misconceptions with examples from my own experience and communicate some of the sense of enjoyment and adventure—and purpose—I share with my colleagues.

Insect collectors seem to share many personality traits in common, but they also exhibit a lot of individuality with respect to choices and priorities. Very often the influence of a mentor or teacher is a strong force that shapes the goals and direction of a beginning student. Sometimes, of course, this influence is minimal, and the student will proceed on his own, perhaps into areas of entomological inquiry often avoided or neglected by others. Indeed, this diversity of choice is fundamental to making amateur entomologists invaluable to their field of study.

Occasionally a collector's priorities will be shaped by a personal challenge. My close friend and colleague of many years, the late L. P. (Paul) Grey, Lincoln, Maine, began collecting butterflies as a youngster and regularly exchanged specimens with collectors throughout North America. A carpenter and tradesman by profession, Paul quickly became exasperated with trying to identify the western fritillaries (genus *Speyeria*). The identifications provided by the "experts" didn't often agree with the pictures in reference books. Paul then began a specialized study (his wife, Ruth, would have called it an obsession) of this genus in North America and related species around the world and soon amassed a huge collection of these butterflies from every nook and cranny of the continent. Paul suspected that the confused taxonomy of the fritillaries was due to the huge diversity of color and pattern exhibited by single species throughout their geographic ranges. Armed with a microscope and determination, Paul undertook, largely on his own, a detailed analysis of the intricate anatomical structures from samples of specimens he received. This study ultimately resulted in a collaborative effort with Cyril F. dos Passos, Mendham, New Jersey, and the publication, in 1947, of their *Systematic Catalogue of Speyeria*. The catalogue reduced more than thirty "species" to a basic thirteen. Paul's subsequent work and expansion of his collection (now housed in the American Museum of Natural History, in New York) further resulted in many additional scientific papers, which form the backbone of our present-day understanding of these butterflies. His abilities at correlating wing color and maculation with geographic region became legendary. It has been said that you could try to lose Paul Grey anywhere in North America without a map or compass and he could tell you exactly where he was by catching and examining a few fritillaries. This is no exaggeration.

I saw him do it with specimens with ambiguous locality data, and the localities were later confirmed! True, Paul was one of a kind, but countless other amateurs have made their own unique contributions to butterfly and moth study. The late Harold M. Bower, Wausau, Wisconsin, restricted nearly all of his collecting to a plot of land surrounding a family lakeside cottage in Oneida County, Wisconsin, where he collected all families of lepidoptera from every available habitat over many years. Much of his collection was later studied by specialists, and at present, some thirty-five years after his death, experts are still finding obscure moth species new to science from this hitherto poorly known region.

Moth collecting, combined with the chase for butterflies, spreads the collector's itinerary around the clock, and the quest for nocturnal species often results in interesting encounters with curious people. Brushes with the law are not uncommon. Many years ago, Wally Morse, then curator of the University of New Hampshire collection, Art Mason, State Entomologist, Don Lennox, and I made an evening collecting trip to Weeks State Park, at Mount Prospect, near Lancaster. We were using "sugar bait" painted on the trees along the roadway and then later checking the spots with flashlights and headlamps to collect the moths attracted to the fermenting mixture. As we were finishing up, a Lancaster police cruiser roared up from out of nowhere, and several officers descended on us, loaded for bear and ready for a real shakedown. Fortunately, the University of New Hampshire boys had their credentials, and the officers reluctantly accepted the fact that we were just harmless bug hunters. It would have been fun to see the station report these gentlemen filed the next day!

Moths, because of the vastly greater numbers of species than their diurnal counterparts, the butterflies, are considerably more challenging to work with and, especially, to identify, because of their typically more obscure colors and patterns. Add to that the small size of the tiny microlepidoptera and the difficulties from sleepless nights, and frayed nerves are compounded. A typical warm evening in late June or July and a mercury vapor light or ultraviolet (black) light will attract a blizzard of nocturnal insects of all orders, and this can have its own hazards. Some years ago, moth expert Dr. Jerry

Powell of the University of California got a small moth lodged in his ear canal and required immediate medical attention. The clinic doctor, unaware of Dr. Powell's expertise, deftly extricated the moth, still alive and kicking, from his ear and was dumbstruck when Powell examined the specimen and blurted out the scientific name. Along with the lighting devices, the old-fashioned method of "sugaring," or baiting, for moths is still popular. A mixture of sugar, fermenting fruit, and an alcoholic additive, such as beer or rum, applied to tree trunks at dusk will attract many species of moths and other insects. This technique would frequently become a social event for the older collectors at the turn of the century. Indeed, the stalwart moth hunters of yesteryear often went into the field equipped to enjoy an evening out, even when collecting was unproductive, and the backwoods cocktail parties of the elder statesmen of entomology are legendary. This practice is, I think, less common today, but I've heard rumors. . . .

As with any other outdoor activity, weather is a constant factor that affects insect collecting, but nowhere is this more dramatic than in the alpine zone of our mountains. The region above tree line is where so many insect species have marvelous adaptations to deal with high winds, sudden drops in temperature, and variable cloud cover, and, just as with plants, the insects adapted for survival at these altitudes are indicative of those of tundra regions. Along our mountain trails the yellow caution signs are not kidding. Inclement weather can occur with incredible swiftness, catching anyone off-guard, including the intrepid insect collector. Some years ago, Jim Holmes and I hiked up Mount Adams for some daytime collecting. The weather was warm and muggy, with plenty of sunshine. Above tree line a good breeze made it considerably cooler, but with the sunshine, insect activity was abundant near the Madison Spring Hut, at an elevation of about 5,000 feet. From the north we noted a good-sized cumulus cloud heading our way, which took on a dark and ominous aspect as it approached and then quickly engulfed the entire mountain. The temperature plunged within seconds, with driving wind and rain that changed to marble-sized hail. We were in the middle of a full-blown thunderhead, and the discharges of lightning were blinding and instantaneously accompanied by earsplitting cracks of thunder. Fortunately for us, two female hikers got trapped in the same spot and generously provided cover for us under a huge tarpaulin they had carried with them. The storm was over in about five minutes, and the four of us crawled out in beautiful sunshine, the ground still white with hailstones. As temperatures quickly warmed, the sudden reappearance of insect life was amazing; butterflies, bees, and day-flying moths busily resumed nectaring over a soaked, hail-studded landscape as though nothing had ever happened. The large rock cairn near where we were minutes before, huddled like frightened rabbits, stood as a blunt reminder: The sign board read LIGHTNING POINT.

My first collecting trip on Mount Washington was with Don Lennox, back in the 1950s, in quest of the White Mountain Butterfly. By day's end we were both sunburned and exhausted. That evening, true to his form, Donald thought it would be great fun to join the merriment at the Jefferson Square Dance Club, so he and his wife, Vivian, dragged me along for an additional new experience. Now, many years later, I still think I can keep up with most of the younger collectors, but believe I'll take a rain check on the dances afterward.

Aside from field collecting and outdoor adventures, keeping and maintaining a large personal collection is a big job, and our long winters provide time for this indoor activity. For studying moths especially, close examination is necessary; in some cases dissections of portions of the anatomy under a microscope are required for proper identification, and these key structures are preserved on microscopic slides. Adding new material and maintaining records in my index file is all part of the job. Still, unidentified species and plenty of loose ends always remain and will provide challenges to future taxonomists and researchers. A vast amount of revisionary work is still needed, especially for the smaller moths, the microlepidoptera, and it's impossible to guess under what new light and insights my material will be seen by future workers. For me, at least, the satisfaction comes with the struggle, and the uncertainty is always part of the adventure. The amateur naturalists of the future, I believe, will experience a good measure of both.

About This Book

In 1901 William Fuller Fiske published *An Annotated Catalog of the Butterflies of New Hampshire*, Technical Bulletin No. 1 of the College of Agriculture and the Mechanical Arts (now University of New Hampshire). This work, now rare and badly out of date, stands as the only comprehensive reference to this state's butterfly fauna. This is rather appalling, considering the diversity of many interesting species native to New Hampshire. In his Harvard University thesis, "The Lepidoptera of New England" (1934), Donald W. Farquhar included many New Hampshire butterfly records, but most of these butterflies are from the southern part of the state. This is unfortunate, as several of the most noteworthy are endemic to the White Mountain region. Our northern region, including upper Grafton and Carroll Counties and all of Coos County to the Canadian border, has received a disproportionately small amount of attention. Since the time of these early lists, a considerable amount of collecting and survey work has been done in our state by amateur and professional entomologists, and the Nature Conservancy and the New Hampshire Natural Heritage Inventory have made an effort to record some of the rarer species of butterflies and moths as a basis for habitat conservation. Still, our state has had relatively few resident collectors, and many parts of New Hampshire, particularly the northern region, remain poorly known.

For nearly forty years I have collected and studied the butterfly and moth fauna of New England, concentrating on northern New Hampshire, where I make my home. During much of this time, I worked with my predecessor and mentor, the late Donald J. Lennox, of Jefferson, a well-known local naturalist who collected butterflies and moths from about 1929 to the late 1960s. His collection, one of the largest and most complete, is now in the entomology collection of the University of New Hampshire. It contains a number of interesting and unusual butterfly records that are cited in this report. James P. Holmes, another Jefferson collector, has accompanied me on countless collecting excursions throughout this region. Other collectors and students, both amateur and professional, have made occasional, sometimes regular, trips to the White Mountains during summer but often miss many species during their brief visits. I have known and corresponded with most of these individuals.

LIFE CYCLE OF THE MOURNING CLOAK BUTTERFLY

1. Mating
2. Laying Eggs
3. Caterpillars Feeding Communally
4. Mature Caterpillars
5. Chrysalis
6. Adult Butterfly

Butterflies and moths belong to the huge insect order Lepidoptera, and their four-stage developmental cycle (complete metamorphosis)—from egg, larva, pupa, to adult insect—is familiar to naturalists. Butterflies occur in nearly every natural environment. Some species have adapted to a wide range of environmental conditions and are generally distributed so that they are well-known and common nearly everywhere. Others have more specialized habits and requirements, and a detailed knowledge of these is necessary before we can become familiar with their diversity in any geographical region.

Our knowledge of butterflies has grown enormously during the last half century, primarily because of the combined efforts of the many professional naturalists and entomologists as well as scores of amateur collectors and students of butterflies who have regularly contributed their findings and observations that are published in scientific periodicals. Several new books on butterflies are now available, so public awareness and appreciation of these insects has greatly increased.

As with other animals, the broad ecological conditions of climate, trees, and herbaceous plants—the so-called faunal life zones—determine the kinds of butterflies one might expect to see in a given region. Within these major life zones, a variety of local habitats reflect local butterfly diversity.

Here in New Hampshire, with its transition from seacoast to inland mountains, the butterfly diversity is substantial, as noted by Weed and Fiske. Even to the casual observer, the topographic and ecological differences between northern and southern New Hampshire are dramatic; our northern part of the state is a different world from the Merrimack Valley or seacoast region. Our considerably higher elevations result in a generally cooler climate and a more northern, or boreal, character to our forests. As one might expect, the butterfly fauna of our area is different in many respects from that in the southern region. Within our area a combination of high mountains, river valleys, mixed deciduous woods and the transition to Canadian-zone forests, and ample marsh and wetland habitats provides habitat for about seventy-five species of butterflies. Most of these species are common to abundant. Several, however, have become rare,

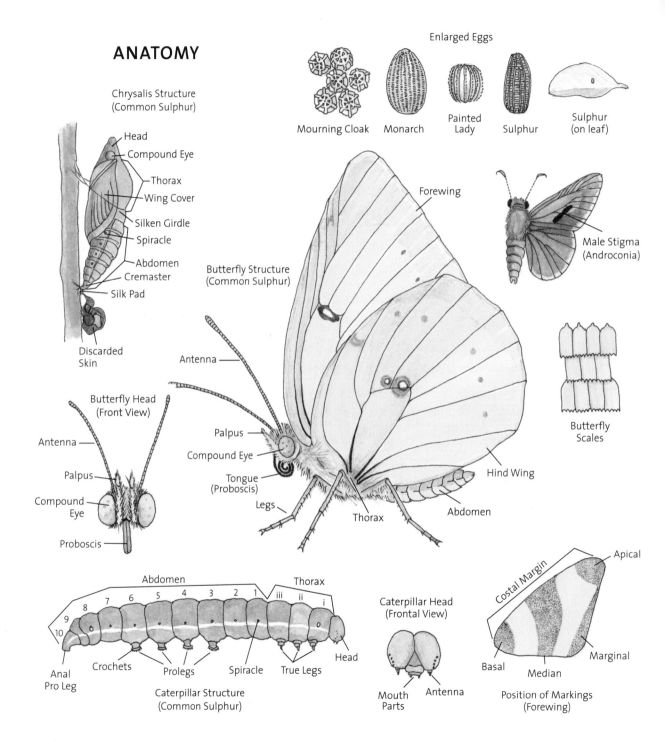

ANATOMY

Enlarged Eggs

Mourning Cloak Monarch Painted Lady Sulphur Sulphur (on leaf)

Chrysalis Structure (Common Sulphur)

Head
Compound Eye
Thorax
Wing Cover
Silken Girdle
Spiracle
Abdomen
Cremaster
Silk Pad
Discarded Skin

Butterfly Structure (Common Sulphur)

Forewing
Male Stigma (Androconia)
Antenna
Hind Wing
Abdomen
Thorax
Legs

Butterfly Head (Front View)

Antenna
Palpus
Compound Eye
Proboscis

Palpus
Compound Eye
Tongue (Proboscis)

Butterfly Scales

Caterpillar Structure (Common Sulphur)

Abdomen
Thorax
10 9 8 7 6 5 4 3 2 1 iii ii i
Anal Pro Leg
Crochets
Prolegs
Spiracle
True Legs
Head

Caterpillar Head (Frontal View)

Mouth Parts
Antenna

Position of Markings (Forewing)

Costal Margin
Apical
Marginal
Median
Basal

and some possibly have disappeared from our area. Several species represent recent additions that have become well established. The fauna of any region is never static, and a list compiled over a long period of time will reflect these changes.

For instance, insect populations often fluctuate dramatically, and many species are sporadic and cyclical. Seasonal weather extremes, disease, predator and parasite buildups, habitat modification, and a host of other factors greatly influence the abundance of species. Natural succession from open farmland to partially grown-in or "old field" conditions to mature forest appears to have affected populations of many generally distributed species.

About this list: All known breeding resident species in the White Mountains region are covered. Each family is briefly described and is then followed by the species entries with detailed information on habits, host plant, and flight period. Unusual records, that is, species of doubtful, casual, or accidental occurrence, are listed in Appendix A.

For some species I've included specific localities where they may be observed. A well-illustrated field guide is almost essential to use with this list, and I've included a selection of general reference works available in most bookstores. Species with special habitat requirements, especially those associated with bogs, wetlands, or other critical environments, are treated in some detail, as these areas usually have unique plants and birds as well as butterflies and are of special interest to students of natural history. The arrangement of species and their scientific names follows the most recently published checklist on butterflies and moths.

The butterflies are worth knowing, and whether one collects and studies them or is content with observing or perhaps photographing them, they remain a colorful and fascinating part of our natural environment. If this list spawns further curiosity or helps someone become more familiar with the butterflies seen along trails, roadways, around woodlands, and in meadows, then it will have served its purpose.

Notes on Specific Habitats

A number of different habitats associated with our butterflies require a bit of elaboration, and, especially for the beginning naturalist, the following practical descriptions may prove useful:

ARCTIC-ALPINE ZONE: Beginning on our highest mountains at an elevation of about 4,500 feet in the White Mountains, this transitional zone occurs from timberline to the tops of our higher peaks. Here tree growth diminishes to gnarled and stunted conditions and gives way to prostrate mats of fir and spruce. At the highest elevations there are only bare, rock-strewn grass and sedge meadows that harbor plant and animal species similar to those on the arctic tundra. From these bleak, windswept regions rise the prominent summit cones. This environment is cold and hostile to most lowland life, but its native plants and animals are uniquely adapted for survival. This zone comprises the upper portion of nearly all of our Presidential Range mountains, and, to a lesser extent, Mount Garfield and Mount Lafayette in the Franconia Range.

ACID BOG: A unique wetland environment, characterized by extreme soil acidity and an ever-encroaching mat of sphagnum moss that often encloses a small lake or pond. Usually rimmed by black spruce saplings and more open toward the center, specialized plants—including pitcher plants, Labrador tea, bog cranberry, leatherleaf, and many heaths and shrubs—thrive in the acid conditions.

OLD FIELD: A term generally used to denote a successional stage of early woodland development, where formerly open fields used for grazing or crops begin to grow up with shrubs, small saplings, and many species of herbaceous plants, grasses, and flowers.

WOODLAND AND FIELD ROADWAYS AND TRAILS: Probably the most accessible to the casual naturalist, these areas are often in proximity to secondary dirt or logging roads, or they adjoin farmlands and open meadows, where one can walk in comfort.

Often a wealth of butterfly species attracted to damp spots and roadside puddles can be observed on sunny days. The most productive woodlands for these observations are mixed deciduous areas. Open, wet sedge meadows and elevated upland fields usually require a departure from the familiar roadsides but will reward the observer with a greater butterfly diversity. Not to be neglected are the woodland margins that border these open areas; they offer partial shade, which is important to a number of butterfly species.

SWAMPS AND WETLANDS: Boots and careful footing are needed in these environments, but occasional access roads will cut very close to or through these areas to minimize the difficulties. Alder thickets, grasses and sedges, turtleheads, and many other wetland plants have associated butterfly species like the Baltimore, Harvester, and Northern Pearly Eye.

Old Fields

Skippers
Family Hesperiidae

Skippers are sometimes considered separately from the true butterflies because of their structure, behavior, and nature of their early stages. They are, however, included in most popular butterfly books. Most skippers are medium-sized to small butterflies with stout bodies, blunt triangular wings, and large, wide heads. The wings are controlled by powerful muscles, permitting a very fast, erratic "skipping" flight, hence the popular name. Some are dark colored, with various shades of brown or black. Others have tawny coloration with dark wing borders, often with pale shades or spots on the underside of the hind wings. The males of many species have sex scales (androconia) concentrated in a dark streak, or "stigma," on the forewings. Nearly all are avid flower visitors, and many are attracted to damp spots along roadways. Most species prefer open fields, roadsides, or sunny clearings, but several favor partial shade near woodland margins. The larvae have smooth, distinctively tapering bodies and when not feeding, usually lie concealed within loose leaf shelters on their host plants. The larvae of most of our species feed on a variety of grasses, but a few feed on leaves of woody shrubs or trees. None of our species is a true wetland endemic, but some are more likely to be seen in or near wetland habitats in association with the larval host plant or favorite flower.

Silver-spotted Skipper

Epargyreus clarus

A large, dark-brownish skipper with a conspicuous silvery-white patch on the underside of the hind wings. Its flight is fast and powerful, and it is often seen visiting many flowers. This species is generally more southern in distribution in the state; it barely enters our area in upper Grafton County and the Conway area eastward. Recent collecting has confirmed this species in the Shelburne area of Coos County and also near the Moore Dam, west of Littleton, from late June to mid-July.

HABITAT: Open fields, roadsides, and woodland clearings.

LARVAL HOST: Black locust. One brood; overwinters as pupa.

WINGTIP SPAN: 1.8–2.0 in. (4.5–5.1 cm)

Northern Cloudy Wing

Thorybes pylades

A large, uniformly dark-colored skipper with a very fast, powerful flight. It is fond of milkweed and many other flowers. It is not widespread in Coos County but is rather common in the Shelburne area.

HABITAT: Open fields and sheltered sunny spots, especially in or near power-line clearings. Adults in mid- to late June.

LARVAL HOST: Clover and other Leguminosae. Probably single brooded in our area; overwinters as pupa.

WINGTIP SPAN: 1.3–1.6 in. (3.3–4.1 cm)

Dreamy Dusky Wing

Erynnis icelus

A very dark, medium-sized skipper with blackish wings with some violet-gray dusting. It is very common locally from late May to early July. It is an avid flower visitor and is also attracted to moist spots along roadways. It often alights on vegetation and usually rests with wings held open.

HABITAT: Open fields, roadsides, and wooded clearings, often favoring more shaded spots than other skippers.

LARVAL HOST: Willows and poplars. One brood; overwinters as pupa.

WINGTIP SPAN: 0.9–1.3 in. (2.3–3.3 cm)

Juvenal's Dusky Wing

Erynnis juvenalis

Similar to other "dusky wing" skippers, with blackish-brown wings, *juvenalis* is rare in Coos County but only because of the lack of scrub oak habitat in that area. It is very common eastward and to the south but may occasionally stray into our area. Flight is from May to early June; it is a strong flyer and is often attracted to flowers.

HABITAT: Open pine and scrub-oak woodlands, typical of much of the country south and east of North Conway.

LARVAL HOST: Scrub oak and other oaks; single brooded. Overwinters as fully-grown larva, pupating in the early spring.

WINGTIP SPAN: 1.2–1.8 in. (3.0–4.5 cm)

Columbine Dusky Wing

Erynnis lucilius

A rare species locally and possibly no longer in our area. It is a very dark-colored skipper, appearing nearly black in flight, but similar to the Dreamy Dusky Wing in habits. Donald J. Lennox reported rearing it in Jefferson many years ago, but I have never taken it or even seen it locally, in spite of numerous searches near its host plant, where it tends to be very localized. This species is apparently uncommon everywhere within its range but is more likely to be seen from southern New England southward. The flight is from late May into July.

HABITAT: Rocky, open woodlands in association with the host plant.

LARVAL HOST: Wild columbine; probably two broods. Local naturalists familiar with this plant should watch for it, and any observations of dark skippers flying near it should be reported. Overwinters as full-grown larva, pupating in early spring.

WINGTIP SPAN: 0.9–1.2 in. (2.3–3.0 cm)

Arctic Skipper

Carterocephalus palaemon

A small, attractive skipper, with a distinctive orange-and-black checkerboard pattern on its upper wings and light spots on the underside of the hind wings. It has a fast, erratic flight, is fond of flowers, and is often attracted to damp spots on trails and roadways, frequently alighting on grasses and other vegetation. Adults fly from early June to early July.

HABITAT: Open, well-lit clearings along woodland trails or wooded edges of meadows an adjacent roadways.

LARVAL HOST: Grasses; single brooded. Overwinters as full-grown larva, pupating in early spring.

WINGTIP SPAN: 0.9–1.1 in. (2.3–2.8 cm)

The Butterflies of the White Mountains

Least Skipper

Ancyloxypha numitor

True to its common name, the Least Skipper is a very small species; it is orange-brown, with darker wing borders. It has a relatively weak flight, low to the ground, and is not widespread in our area but is rather limited to its habitat. Flight is from late June through July and again in August.

HABITAT: Open, moist meadows with an abundance of tall grasses, where it occurs in small, local colonies.

LARVAL HOST: Grasses; two broods. Overwinters as partly grown larva.

WINGTIP SPAN: 0.8–1.0 in. (2.0–2.5 cm)

European Skipper

Thymelicus lineola

The European Skipper is a relatively recent addition to our butterfly fauna. It was originally introduced from Europe in London, Ontario, around 1910 and has been gradually spreading throughout the northeast. Since its first appearance in Coos County in 1982, it has become prolific and is now perhaps our most common skipper. Its range continues to expand throughout North America. It is a medium-sized, bright golden orange-brown skipper with a somewhat sluggish flight. It is fond of many flowers, especially purple vetch and milkweed. Flight period is from late June to mid-July.

HABITAT: Any open sunny areas, fields, and roadsides that have an abundance of flowers.

LARVAL HOST: Grasses; one brood locally. Overwinters in the egg stage.

WINGTIP SPAN: 0.8–1.1 in. (2.0–2.8 cm)

Laurentian Skipper

Hesperia comma laurentina

Our Laurentian Skipper is a geographic race or subspecies of *Hesperia comma,* a well-known species that occurs throughout much of Europe and western North America. It was first collected in New Hampshire in the Pittsburg area around 1966 by Donald J. Lennox, of Jefferson, and Wallace J. Morse, then curator of the University of New Hampshire entomology collection. It appears to have spread southward from Canada and is now one of our most common skippers. It is an attractive tawny orange-brown species with dark wing borders above; the underside of the hind wing is light greenish with white spots. It has a fast flight and is very common from early to late August. An avid flower visitor, it is especially attracted to flat-topped goldenrod.

HABITAT: Fields, open meadows, and roadsides.

LARVAL HOST: Various grasses; single brooded. In New England, probably overwinters as egg. May overwinter as older larva or pupa in Arctic regions.

WINGTIP SPAN: 0.9–1.3 in. (2.3–3.3 cm)

Leonard's Skipper

Hesperia leonardus

Although common in parts of the northeast, Leonard's Skipper is apparently quite rare in the White Mountains. My only capture record is a single specimen, collected 19 August 1966, on the Bray Hill Road between Jefferson and Whitefield. It is similar to the Laurentian Skipper but is larger and darker; underneath, the hind wing is light brown with several light spots. Adults fly from mid-August through September and actively visit many kinds of flowers. It is sometimes associated with open areas near wetlands.

HABITAT: Open fields, damp meadows, and along dirt roads near wetlands.

LARVAL HOST: Various grasses. Single brooded; overwinters as a partly grown larva.

WINGTIP SPAN: 1.1–1.4 in. (2.8–3.6 cm)

Indian Skipper

Hesperia sassacus

Not widespread in northern New Hampshire but occasionally seen in local colonies. It is smaller and brighter orange-brown than Leonard's Skipper, but, like others of this genus, the males have a forewing stigma streak. It has a typical erratic, fast flight and is fond of many flowers. Flight period is throughout June into early July.

HABITAT: Upland open fields and meadows. I have taken it locally in power-line clearings.

LARVAL HOST: Grasses. One brood; overwinters as pupa.

WINGTIP SPAN: 1.0–1.4 in. (2.5–3.6 cm)

Peck's Skipper

Polites peckius

A very common, small skipper with a typical tawny-and-brown pattern above and a conspicuous yellow patch on the underside of the hind wings. It is attracted to many kinds of flowers, especially purple vetch. Adults fly from late May into July.

HABITAT: Open fields, meadows, and roadsides; virtually any open area with an abundance of flowers.

LARVAL HOST: Grasses; at least one brood and possibly a partial second. Overwinters as larva or pupa.

WINGTIP SPAN: 0.9–1.0 in. (2.3–2.5 cm)

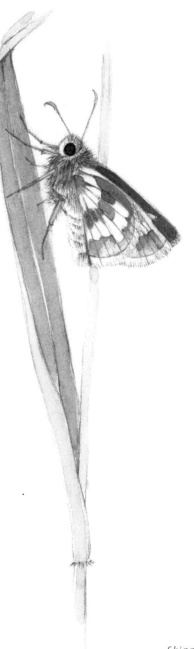

Tawny-edged Skipper

Polites themistocles

Wings are a dark olive-brown above with a tawny yellow-brown shading along the front edge of the forewings. The males have a stigma patch; females tend to be uniformly dark with pale forewing spots. A strong, fast flyer. Like most skippers it is attracted to flowers, purple vetch being a favorite. Adults are active from mid-June to early July and are abundant in our area.

HABITAT: Open fields, meadows, and roadsides.

LARVAL HOST: Grasses; one brood; probably overwinters as pupa.

WINGTIP SPAN: 0.8–1.1 in. (2.0–2.8 cm)

The Long Dash

Polites mystic

Another abundant species. Males have an elongated dark-brown streak or shading beyond the forewing stigma, giving this species its popular name. As with most of the other field skippers, the females tend to have darker, more suffused coloration. Fond of purple vetch, milkweed, and many other flowers, adults are active from early June to late July.

HABITAT: As with the other skippers, sunny open fields and meadows.

LARVAL HOST: Grasses; single brooded in our area. Overwinters as fourth-stage larva.

WINGTIP SPAN: 1.0–1.3 in. (2.5–3.3 cm)

Hobomok Skipper

Poanes hobomok

A very common early summer species, tawny golden-brown above with contrasting dark borders and a large yellow patch on the underside of the hind wings. The males of this genus lack the forewing stigma mark, but, as with the others, the females are darker colored. A rare, even darker color form of the female is named *pocahontas*, with the underside yellow patch replaced by violet-gray shading. It visits flowers freely and is on the wing from mid-June to early July.

HABITAT: Most often seen near woodland clearings or in fields near edges of woods and thickets, often alighting on foliage.

LARVAL HOST: Grasses; single brooded. Overwinters as chrysalis or larva.

WINGTIP SPAN: 1.1–1.3 in. (2.8–3.3 cm)

Eastern Dun Skipper

Euphyes vestris

A very dark, uniformly blackish-brown species; females have faint buff-colored forewing spots. Moderately common in the White Mountains and an avid flower visitor, it is seen from late June to early August.

HABITAT: Open fields, damp meadows, and roadsides.

LARVAL HOST: Sedges; single brooded. Overwinters as third-stage larva.

WINGTIP SPAN: 1.1–1.3 in. (2.8–3.3 cm)

Pepper and Salt Skipper

Amblyscirtes hegon

One of our smallest skippers, *hegon* was originally described by
Dr. Samuel H. Scudder in 1864. It is blackish-brown above with a
few obscure pale spots; the underside of the hind wings is
dusted with greenish-gray with some light spots. It has an
erratic, fast flight, low to the ground. It is fond of some flowers
but is more likely to be seen around the gravelly edges of dirt
roads where there are puddles or moist spots and plenty of
nearby grasses and sedges. Flight is from late May to mid-July; it
is a common early summer species.

HABITAT: Along dirt roads, as described above, and occasionally
in open fields, where the common blue aster is a favorite flower.

LARVAL HOST: Grasses. Larva has been reared on *Poa pratensis;*
one brood in our area. Overwinters as larva.

WINGTIP SPAN: 0.8–1.1 in. (2.0–2.8 cm)

Roadside Skipper

Amblyscirtes vialis

Similar to the Pepper and Salt Skipper, but darker; nearly black above, with faint light spots near the wing tips; the underside of the hind wing is shaded with violet-gray. It has a rapid, erratic flight, low to the ground, and is very common in early summer, from late May to mid-June. It visits a variety of flowers but seems especially fond of blueberry blossoms.

HABITAT: Sometimes seen in fields, especially near the edges of woods, or along open roadways.

LARVAL HOST: Grasses, especially of the genus *Poa*. One brood. Overwinters as chrysalis.

WINGTIP SPAN: 0.8–1.1 in. (2.0–2.8 cm)

Woodland Roadways
and Trails

Swallowtails

Family Papilionidae

The swallowtails, aptly named for their hind-wing appendages, are the largest and most conspicuous butterflies. Well-known to most people as harbingers of summer, with their majestic and graceful flight they're always a delight to see after a long winter, especially around our gardens and flowering shrubs. They are, for the most part, a temperate and tropical family of butterflies, and we have only two species that are regular breeding residents here in the White Mountains.

Swallowtails are avid flower visitors, and some species are frequently seen in large numbers congregating at mud puddles along dirt roads, as with our common Canadian Tiger Swallowtail. The larvae feed on a wide variety of trees, shrubs, and herbaceous plants, and they are smooth-skinned and variously colored, with distinctive patterns for most species. All larvae possess scent organs (osmataria) behind the head, which, when extended, give off a strong odor as a deterrent to predators.

Of our two species, only the Canadian Tiger Swallowtail occurs in noticeable abundance. The Black Swallowtail used to be more common than at present but is still seen occasionally during the summer months.

Two species that do not normally occur in the White Mountains have been collected here: the Pipevine and Spicebush Swallowtails. These species occur typically in central New England and southward, and two unusual Jefferson records for these are discussed in Appendix A.

Black Swallowtail

Papilio polyxenes

This "common" Black Swallowtail is no longer common in the White Mountains. Although it has never been abundant, I can recall seeing greater numbers of them coursing over open fields and meadows back in the 1950s. I don't know the reasons for its decline, but the loss of open country may be a factor. It is nearly all black, with a double row of yellow spots near the wing margins. It is fond of flowers; cultivated phlox, common in many residential gardens, is a favorite. Dr. Donald Miller, zoologist at Lyndon State College, in Vermont, reports that it is fairly common in an open swampy area near Lyndonville, although it certainly isn't associated with wetlands. It may be seen in any favorable open area from June through August.

HABITAT: Fields and general open areas; occasionally seen in gardens.

LARVAL HOST: A wide variety of wild and cultivated Umbelliferae: caraway, Queen Anne's lace, carrot, parsley, celery, dill, and the like. Two broods; overwinters as pupa.

WINGTIP SPAN: 2.5–3.2 in. (6.4–8.1 cm)

The Butterflies of the White Mountains

Canadian Tiger Swallowtail

Papilio canadensis

Our abundant yellow-and-black Tiger Swallowtail, which
is a familiar sight everywhere from late May into July,
hardly needs a description. Until very recently it was
thought to be a northern race or subspecies of the
Eastern Tiger Swallowtail, *Papilio glaucus,* which is widely
distributed throughout eastern North America. Research,
however, has shown that because of slightly different
flight periods, host-plant selection, and, particularly, color
and pattern differences of newly hatched larvae,
northern New England populations represent a very
close but distinct species. Although our northern species
has nearly identical markings, it is slightly smaller and
paler and flies earlier in the season than the Eastern
Tiger. Recent collecting by Dr. Donald Miller indicates
that the Eastern Tiger Swallowtail does occur in New
Hampshire, at least as far north as Hillsborough County,
but it is not known exactly where the ranges of the two
species connect, or if there is an appreciable area of
overlap. During late spring large numbers of males of
our Canadian Tiger Swallowtail may be seen along dirt

roads congregating at puddles and damp spots. In 1995 enormous numbers were observed "puddling" in many locations. A particularly large aggregation was observed in June along the damp roadside edges in a clearing along the Dartmouth College Grant Road, in Wentworth Location. The butterflies were resting and feeding, tightly packed side by side, for a distance of 20 or 30 feet along the roadway where the swamp slightly overflows; a very loose estimate would be 600 or 700 individuals, the largest number of these butterflies I've ever seen in one place. As I walked slowly beside this shimmering colony, each butterfly rose into the air, continuing to soar and circle around the spot. After "walking the gauntlet," I stood in the middle of the roadway amid a swirling maelstrom of swallowtails—overwhelming from my perspective, and a spectacular photo, had someone been present with a camera.

HABITAT: Open and partially shaded areas everywhere, along roadways and watersheds, and especially residential gardens, where they are particularly attracted to lilac and honeysuckle blossoms.

LARVAL HOST: Lilac, cherry, poplar, and ash. One brood; overwinters as pupa.

WINGTIP SPAN: 2.8–3.3 in. (7.1–8.4 cm)

Alpine Zone

Whites and Sulphurs

Family Pieridae

Whites and sulphurs are conspicuous because of their light coloration, which is usually some shade of white, yellow, or orange without many additional markings. Of our two species of whites, one, the Cabbage White, is a well-known economic pest of many garden crops and plants. Our sulphurs are bright yellow or orange (females have occasional white forms), and all of our native species have dark-brown or blackish-brown wing borders on the upper side. All are medium-sized butterflies and are commonly seen in fields and along roadsides. Although many North American species favor temperate and subtropical environments, a few species of sulphurs are denizens of the alpine zones in western mountainous areas or northern tundra barrens. Males and females almost always have slightly different wing patterns (sexual dimorphism) or changes evidenced in seasonal broods (seasonal dimorphism). The larvae of many species are greenish in color and feed on a wide variety of plants, mostly low, herbaceous plants in the pea and mustard families in the case of our native species. Some are noted for their migratory habits, and at least one southern species, described in Appendix A, occasionally enters coastal New England and even up into the White Mountains. Our whites and sulphurs are attracted to many kinds of flowers, and large numbers of sulphurs are often seen congregating at mud puddles and damp spots along roadways.

Mustard White

Pieris oleracea

A nearly all-white butterfly common throughout most of the summer. In the spring color form, which flies from around mid-May to mid-June, the underside of the hind wings has dark-gray coloration along the veins. In the late summer form, appearing from mid- to late July, this gray coloration is much reduced. This is our only native white and, although still quite common, is much less abundant since the Cabbage White was introduced around 1860. As both species share similar host plants, many experts think that competition has favored the Cabbage White, forcing the native species into increasing seclusion northward and restricting it to more heavily wooded areas. In these areas it is usually very common, especially along the Dartmouth Grant's Hellgate Road, in Wentworth Location.

HABITAT: Moist deciduous woodlands, especially in clearings and along dirt roads.

LARVAL HOST: The native wild host is toothwort *(Dentaria)*, a common plant along woodland streams and moist areas. Other plants include rock cresses, water cresses, and wild and cultivated Cruciferae. I have reared it successfully on turnip and cabbage. Two broods in our area; overwinters as pupa.

WINGTIP SPAN: 1.3–1.6 in. (3.3–4.1 cm)

The Butterflies of the White Mountains

Cabbage White
Pieris rapae

Nearly everyone is familiar with the destructive potential of this species, which has spread throughout most of North America since its introduction from Europe into Quebec around 1860. It flies from early spring to early fall, becoming extremely abundant in late summer, when our gardens mature. The ravages of the larvae, or "cabbage worms," can be seen on a wide variety of crop plants. The pattern of black spots on the wings is seasonally variable; late summer individuals are more heavily marked. It occurs in virtually every environment but is especially abundant in open areas. The Cabbage White is attracted to many flowers.

HABITAT: Nearly all open country, cultivated rural areas, and suburbs, where residential gardens provide so many food sources for the larvae.

LARVAL HOST: Nearly all wild and cultivated Cruciferae: cabbage, mustard, turnip, broccoli, nasturtium, spider flower, and many others. Three broods; overwinters as pupa.

WINGTIP SPAN: 1.3–1.8 in. (3.3–4.6 cm)

Clouded Sulphur

Colias philodice

The Clouded Sulphur is widespread and abundant nearly everywhere throughout most of North America; it is clear yellow, with dark-brown wing borders above in the males and darker, broken borders in the females. It is commonly seen at many flowers, especially clover, when it swarms in numbers over open fields during summer. "Puddling" aggregations of many individuals are often noted. It flies from late spring throughout summer, often into late fall. White forms of the females are not uncommon, the yellow replaced with white coloration but with normal dark borders.

HABITAT: Fields and meadows; nearly every open environment.

LARVAL HOST: Clovers, vetch, lupine, alfalfa, and other Leguminosae. Three broods; overwinters as pupa, sometimes as adult or larva.

WINGTIP SPAN: 1.3–1.9 in. (3.3–4.8 cm)

Orange Sulphur

Colias eurytheme

Common in our area throughout summer into mid-autumn and distinguished by predominately orange color on the wings above with dark-brown borders. It is very closely related to *philodice,* and intermediate color forms between *eurytheme* and *philodice* have fueled speculation about the possibility of hybridization. Like the Clouded Sulphur, the Orange Sulphur frequently produces white females with normal dark wing borders. This species also is fond of clover blossoms and other flowers.

HABITAT: Open fields and meadows, generally distributed everywhere.

LARVAL HOST: Alfalfa, white and other clovers, vetch, lupine, and the like. At least two broods in our area; overwinters as pupa, perhaps also as adult.

WINGTIP SPAN: 1.6–2.4 in. (4.1–6.1 cm)

The Butterflies of the White Mountains

Pink-edged Sulphur

Colias interior

Very similar to the Clouded Sulphur and nearly indistinguishable in flight, the conspicuous pink wing fringes give this species its common name. In our area it flies from early to late July, is attracted to many kinds of flowers, and is especially common in upland fields and meadows with an abundance of blueberry, the larval host plant. Quite often it is seen around open mountain ledges, where blueberry frequently grows in profusion near rocky outcroppings or even above the timberline. It flies with a little more energy than the Clouded Sulphur, and large numbers occasionally congregate at puddles or damp spots on the ground.

HABITAT: Open fields and meadows, especially those with blueberry.

LARVAL HOST: Blueberries. One brood; overwinters as larva.

WINGTIP SPAN: 1.3–1.8 in. (3.3–4.6 cm)

Acid Bog

Blues, Coppers, and Hairstreaks

Family Lycaenidae

This large family contains our smallest butterflies, and although the majority of them occur in more temperate and tropical regions, we have some interesting species as breeding residents here in the White Mountains. Many species are noted for their metallic or iridescent colors, although the elfins, a closely related group, are rather dark and drab. Nearly all are avid flower visitors, and many species are attracted to damp spots along trails and roadways. The larvae tend to be stout and sluglike, and most feed on a variety of plants, some species preferring the flower buds rather than the foliage. The caterpillars of many tend to be cannibalistic, and the larva of one species, Harvester, is a predator on white woolly aphids. The larvae of some of the blues secrete, from internal glands, "honeydew," which attracts ants that feed on this substance; the ants provide the larvae with protection—a typical symbiotic or mutually beneficial, relationship.

Nearly all our species in this family occur in open environments. The Bog Copper, however, is strictly limited to wetlands and bogs in close association with the bog cranberry, its host plant.

The Butterflies of the White Mountains

Harvester

Feniseca tarquinius

Although not confined to wetlands, the Harvester is often seen in swampy areas near growths of alder. This little orange-brown and black butterfly lays its eggs in masses of white woolly aphids, or plant lice, that feed in conspicuous clumps on the branches of alder. The larvae remain imbedded in the aphid mass, feeding on these insects and maturing very quickly. The chrysalis, or pupa, of the Harvester is one of the more unusual objects in nature; when viewed from behind, it resembles a little "monkey face." This butterfly isn't much of a flower visitor but has an active, erratic flight and often alights on alder foliage. A typical location, where I have seen them in numbers, is along the roadway between the Whitefield Airport and the power lines near the beaver dam at the east end of the runway. I found them to be quite common here in 1972. Adults fly from early June to late July.

HABITAT: Swampy woodland edges and clearings near alder and along roadways adjacent to these environments.

LARVAL HOST: Various species of woolly aphids of the genera *Schizoneura* and *Pemphigus*, primarily on alder, but found on other plants as well. Overwinters as pupa, perhaps also as adult; several broods.

WINGTIP SPAN: 1.3 in. (3.3 cm)

American Copper

Lycaena phlaeas americana

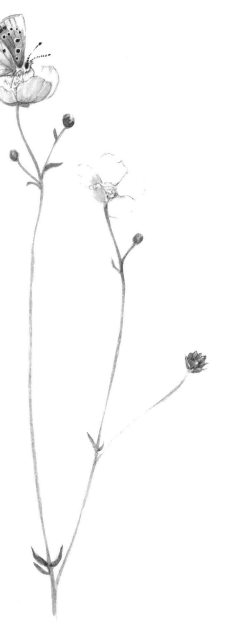

Common in parts of Europe, the subspecies name *americana* applies to North American populations. The distribution of this butterfly is quite remarkable. The range maps in *The Butterflies of North America*, by James A. Scott, show that although it is common throughout most of the eastern United States and southeastern Canada (rare in the South and West), it also has huge disjunct populations near the top of the continent and beyond. This includes most of Baffin Island, the western tip of Greenland, and a small portion through British Columbia clear to the north shores of Alaska, with large gaps in between— quite a legacy of adaptation for a delicate little butterfly. Here in northern New Hampshire, it is quite common in open meadows and upland fields, and, like most coppers, has an erratic "flickering" flight. It is fond of many flowers and is likely to be seen from late May to early October. Above, the wings are deep coppery-orange with a few black spots and dark-brown borders with much light-gray coloration beneath.

HABITAT: Meadows and upland "old fields."

LARVAL HOST: Field or sheep sorrel. Two broods; overwinters as pupa.

WINGTIP SPAN: 1.0 in. (2.5 cm)

Bronze Copper

Lycaena hyllus

Although common throughout the Northeast and parts of the American West, I have never seen nor collected the Bronze Copper in northern New Hampshire. Donald Lennox, however, took it in Jefferson many years ago. I have taken it in Barre and Marshfield, Vermont, and my impression is that it seems to favor open country with an abundance of fields and meadows. In northern New Hampshire large tracts of forest have filled in much of what was once open farmland, and it is possible that this has affected the habitat potential for this butterfly. It is the largest of our native coppers, with coppery-brown wings above and an orange band at the margin of the hind wing; beneath it is paler and spotted with black. Adults fly in mid-June and again in mid-August and are fond of many field and roadside flowers.

HABITAT: Open fields, moist meadows, and roadsides.

LARVAL HOST: Yellow dock, knotweed. Two broods; overwinters as egg.

WINGTIP SPAN: 1.3–1.4 in. (3.3–3.6 cm)

Bog Copper

Lycaena epixanthe

An extremely local species, strictly limited to acid bog habitats and closely associated with growths of bog cranberry, the larval host plant. The males are dark purplish-brown above, and the females, as with most coppers, are more dull in color. Beneath, the wings are contrasting light gray tinged with yellow. These colors, combined with an erratic, elusive flight close to the ground, make it difficult to follow with the eye. Populations of this species seem to favor the wetter bogs, usually those incompletely filled in by the sphagnum rim with a central pond of water. Mud Pond, located between Whitefield and Jefferson, has a bog rim that supports a colony of this butterfly, as does the Pondicherry Refuge's Little Cherry Pond. These very wet, highly acidic rims of ponds and small lakes allow the most favorable growing conditions for bog cranberry, and the butterfly is always found close by. Although it is considered an obligate bog species, there is some evidence to suggest that the Bog Copper and other habitat-restricted species are capable of dispersing occasionally and recolonizing adjacent favorable areas. Whether or not they do this on a regular or random basis is not known. Noted butterfly authority Professor Alexander B. Klots has pointed out that over very long periods of time, such bogs tend to become less favorable for such species as the Bog Copper, as the

ever-enlarging sphagnum mat rims fill in the ponds. The natural succession of different plants and a general drying out create an increasingly less suitable environment for endemic species; therefore, it seems likely that if a species is sufficiently adaptable to make such transitions successfully, this would be a positive factor in terms of its long-term survival.

The Bog Copper flies from early July into late August, and colonies are more active late in the afternoon than during the hot part of the day. It is fond of flowers, and a number of bog plants in bloom at this time provide a nectar source.

HABITAT: Open portions of sphagnum bogs, always very near where bog cranberry grows in abundance. One brood; overwinters as egg, which is able to survive in winter floods.

LARVAL HOST: Bog cranberry *(Vaccinium oxycoccus)*.

WINGTIP SPAN: 0.9 in. (2.3 cm)

Coral Hairstreak

Satyrium titus

Hairstreaks are closely related to the coppers and blues, and most species have short, fragile, threadlike "tails" at the rear portion of the hind wings. The Coral Hairstreak, however, like a number of others, lacks these appendages. Hairstreaks generally are a rather dull brownish-gray on the upper side of the wings, often with a bit of orange and/or blue-gray color at the rear of the hind wings. The underside colors and patterns are more complex and distinct enough between species so that they may be differentiated. The Coral Hairstreak is rather sporadic in the White Mountains, and some years I don't see it at all. It was quite common in a field near my house in Whitefield in 1990. It is completely dark brown above and brownish-gray beneath, with a tapering band of coral-orange near the hind-wing margins. As with all hairstreaks, the flight is swift and darting, and it favors open fields and clearings. It is an avid flower visitor. In our area adults fly in late July into early August.

HABITAT: Open meadows and upland "old fields."

LARVAL HOST: Wild cherry, plum. One brood; overwinters as egg.

WINGTIP SPAN: 1.0–1.1 in. (2.5–2.8 cm)

Acadian Hairstreak

Satyrium acadica

Like most of the hairstreaks that occur in the White Mountains, the Acadian Hairstreak is not common. It tends to be sporadic and local, appearing in small numbers in a particular spot, then perhaps is not seen again for a season or more. It is one of the "tailed" hairstreaks; dark gray-brown above, lighter underneath, with a thin marginal band of red on the hind wings followed by blue-gray patches of color. It has a typical elusive, darting flight and is fond of flowers, especially milkweed and joe-pye-weed blossoms. In our area adults fly in late July.

HABITAT: Wet meadows and along streams where there are willows.

LARVAL HOST: Various willows. One brood; overwinters as egg.

WINGTIP SPAN: 1.2 in. (3.0 cm)

Banded Hairstreak

Satyrium calanus

This is the only hairstreak I've seen consistently in numbers in fairly predictable locations. It occurs almost always near oak trees, the larval host plant. Another typically "tailed" hairstreak, it is dark blackish-brown above, dark gray-brown beneath, with a double row, or "bands," of black dashes edged with white. From mid-July to early August, this species is often seen near sunny clearings or wooded edges of fields near an abundant quantity of oaks. Like other hairstreaks they can be very territorial; during their courtship flights, they will aggressively chase one another or even attack other butterflies, often returning to their same perch on oak leaves or other vegetation. They are also very fond of flowers, particularly meadowsweet and milkweed.

HABITAT: Clearings and fields near oak woods.

LARVAL HOST: Various oaks, probably red oak in northern New Hampshire. One brood; overwinters as egg.

WINGTIP SPAN: 1.0–1.5 in. (2.5–2.9 cm)

Striped Hairstreak

Satyrium liparops

The undersides of both wings of this hairstreak have parallel sets of fine, dark, vertical lines edged with white, giving them a striped appearance. Most often seen in open fields and meadows, visiting milkweed, meadowsweet, or other flowers, it flies from late June to early August. It is fairly common in our area, and a large variety of plants and trees serve as larval hosts. This species also has tails present on the hind wings.

HABITAT: Open fields, especially "old fields" and meadows.

LARVAL HOST: A wide variety, including oak, willow, shadbush, apple, plum, blueberry, blackberry, and the like. One brood; overwinters in the egg stage.

WINGTIP SPAN: 1.2 in. (3.0 cm)

Brown Elfin

Callophrys augustinus

The elfins are like hairstreaks in many respects and are closely related to them. The chief difference is their lack of tails, the margins of the hind wings being rather strongly scalloped. The upper-wing colors are drab, blackish-brown in the males, with a slight reddish flush in the females. The underside of the hind wings has a conspicuous, irregular band, separating lighter and darker shades, and, for a couple of species, several wavy scalloped bands of contrasting brown or grayish color. As with the hairstreaks, the variation in these intricate patterns enables students to identify the species. The elfins fly early in spring, and all the species are single brooded. The Brown Elfin is among the first spring butterflies, appearing in early to mid-May and flying into early June. Open upland fields, especially near growths of blueberries, are particularly favorable habitats, and it freely comes to the flowers of these and other low plants. It is also commonly seen in bogs, as flowering heaths provide nectar sources.

HABITAT: Any open fields or clearings, especially with an abundance of blueberry.

LARVAL HOST: Blueberry, sheep laurel. One brood; overwinters as pupa.

WINGTIP SPAN: 0.9–1.0 in. (2.3–2.5 cm)

Eastern Pine Elfin

Callophrys niphon

Much larger than the Brown Elfin, the Pine Elfin has several scalloped bands of deep brown on the hind wings beneath, with shades of buff and gray coloration in between. The females tend to be shaded with reddish-brown above. Its abundance varies; it is uncommon in some years and very common in others. As the name suggests, it is associated with habitats near pine woods, as pine is the larval host. Like all elfins it has an aggressive hairstreaklike flight. Blueberry blossoms are also a favorite nectar source for this species, as these plants are so often associated with pineland habitat. It flies from May into June and is often seen in company with the Brown Elfin.

HABITAT: In clearings and along roadways near stands of white pine.

LARVAL HOST: Pine, perhaps several species. Single brooded. Overwinters as pupa.

WINGTIP SPAN: 0.8–1.2 in. (2.0–3.1 cm)

Western Pine Elfin

Callophrys eryphon

In the spring of 1975, amateur collectors caught some unusually marked Pine Elfins south of Wilsons Mills, in western Maine. Superficially, these examples, taken in a small roadside bog, resembled the Eastern Pine Elfin but with underside wing markings quite atypical for our familiar species. Specimens were sent to Dr. Harry K. Clench, at the Carnegie Museum of Natural History, in Pittsburgh, Pennsylvania, who confirmed that they were not the typical Eastern Pine Elfin but indeed represented an extreme eastern population of the Western Pine Elfin, which typically occurs from the Rocky Mountains westward. Subsequently, other colonies of this little "displaced" butterfly were discovered in Quebec, and, in June 1995, I captured a single example on the Dartmouth College Grant Road, Wentworth Location, on the New Hampshire side. Additional small colonies of it have recently been discovered in other locations in western Maine.

Here in northern New Hampshire the two species fly about the same time, from late May to early June.

HABITAT: Clearings in or around bogs or low, swampy habitats, usually near stands of pine, nearby open fields, or along roadways in the vicinity.

LARVAL HOST: Eastern pine and perhaps other pines. Single brooded; overwinters as pupa.

WINGTIP SPAN: 0.9–1.1 in. (2.3–2.8 cm)

Gray Hairstreak

Strymon melinus

Ranging from southern Canada throughout the United States and into tropical America, this most "common" of hairstreaks is not at all common in northern New Hampshire, although I do see it occasionally. It is very dark gray above, much lighter gray beneath, with a bit of orange color at the rear portion of upper- and lower-hind surfaces. It has a swift, darting flight and visits many kinds of flowers from early to late summer. The apparent scarcity of this species in Coos County is a puzzle, as it is generally distributed and considered common throughout the Northeast. In fact, until July 1994, I had no local records of this species, although Don Lennox apparently took it here years ago. Leave it to a tourist, however, to come up with a new butterfly record for my list! I was collecting with Edgar Cohen and his wife, who were visiting from Maryland, and we had stopped at a spot along the upper Hazen Road just outside Whitefield. Edgar spotted a little butterfly on a flower and jumped for his net. I was speechless when he told me what he'd caught and had to leave to him the explanation of how he had managed to snag a species that the "local expert" had failed to notice all these years!

HABITAT: Open fields, upland "old fields," roadside clearings.

LARVAL HOST: Hops, mallow, knotweed, Saint-John's-wort, cultivated beans, hawthorn, and many others. It is sometimes a pest on hop or bean crops. Two broods; overwinters as pupa.

WINGTIP SPAN: 1.1 in. (2.8 cm)

Early Hairstreak

Erora laeta

This tailless hairstreak is the great prize of northeastern butterfly collectors. For generations it has been considered a great rarity, but observations in recent years have shown it to be much more common than previously supposed. *Erora* is a tropical genus, and, as only two species are represented in North America, our very limited knowledge of the behavior and biology of *laeta* has spawned many misconceptions about its relative abundance. True to its name, it flies much earlier than the more common hairstreaks; on average, from about mid- to late May. Its color and pattern also set it apart from most hairstreaks. Above, the males are brownish-black, with a bit of deep blue iridescence on the rear portion of the hind wing; the females are a deep, iridescent blue on both wings, with wide dark borders. The underside of both sexes is a very pale gray-green with double rows of coral-colored spots on the hind wings. Its habitat is equally unique; it is almost always associated with partially shaded trails and clearings in beech woods. It is suspected, although probably unconfirmed, that *laeta* has essentially a treetop existence, descending from the canopy only on rare occasions. Most often, single sightings or captures are reported, but in some parts of the Northeast, great numbers of them have been observed at ground level in beech woods, usually at moist spots along trails and pathways warmed by patches of sunlight. During the past fifteen years or so, I have seen small numbers of them on only one

occasion, along an old annex road near the Dolly Copp Campground, south of Gorham. I also have a single capture record of it from the junction of Wesson and Prospect Roads, in Lancaster. In both instances the habitat was one of mixed hardwoods where beech predominated. In the past collectors have taken or observed it in a number of other locations in Coos County. Aspects of *laeta*'s life history have been likewise enigmatic. Beech, the long-suspected host plant for this species, has been confirmed on a number of occasions, but laboratory rearings on hazel (*Corylus*), one species of oak (*Quercus*), and willow (*Salix*) have also been successful. Many years ago, Donald J. Lennox, of Jefferson, observed female *laeta* laying eggs on beaked hazelnut (*Corylus cornuta*) in Jefferson Notch and reared several larvae to the pupa stage, which did not successfully emerge into adults. Reginald Webster, New Brunswick, Canada, recently informed me of places there where *laeta* occurs in great numbers. He has observed females laying eggs on young, developing beechnuts and discovered that the newly hatched larvae fed on the fuzz of the seed husks. More collecting and life-history work are sure to turn up interesting facts about this perplexing butterfly.

HABITAT: Almost exclusively shaded trails and roadways in and around beech woods, although there have been a few curious exceptions.

LARVAL HOST: Certainly American beech, beaked hazelnut, and, most likely, several other plants within our region. Probably double brooded, although second brood (July) records are scarce. Overwinters as pupa.

WINGTIP SPAN: 0.8–0.9 in. (2.0–2.3 cm)

Eastern Tailed-Blue

Everes comyntas

Our only blue with tiny hairstreaklike "tails" on the hind wings, the Eastern Tailed-Blue is much less common in northern New Hampshire than farther south, but it does occur here with some regularity. It is most likely to be seen from mid- to late summer in a variety of open environments with abundant flowers. The nearly all-blue upper-wing colors of the male make it easily confused with the late-summer brood of the much more common Spring Azure. The females, however, differ from the Azure in being nearly all dark grayish-brown above. In Coos County I have seen it from late July into early October in such varied habitats as the alpine zone of the Presidential Range and on Mount Lafayette in Franconia, as well as in lowland open fields and in at least one bog environment.

HABITAT: Any sunny open area with flowers.

LARVAL HOST: Various Leguminosae: clover, milk pea, false indigo, tick trefoils, and others. At least two broods. Overwinters as larva within legume pod.

WINGTIP SPAN: 0.9–1.1 in. (2.3–2.8 cm)

Spring Azure

Celastrina ladon

Our abundant and well-known blue, the Spring Azure, hardly needs an introduction to naturalists; to even the untrained eye, this little butterfly flitting over a still-browned winter landscape in early spring truly signals the end of another long, cold New England winter. The males are bright blue above, and the females have brownish-black borders on the forewings. Both sexes are pale grayish-white beneath, with darker spots and markings. The early spring population hatches from overwintered pupae, flying from about the first week of May into June; the second brood flies from mid-July into August.

HABITAT: Occurs nearly everywhere: clearings and thickets, often along roadways through wooded areas, where adults are attracted to damp spots and puddles, and in fields along woodland edges, where they often fly well up from ground level.

LARVAL HOST: Flowering and other dogwoods, black snakeroot, meadowsweet, and many others, the larvae often eating the flower buds. Two broods; overwinters as pupa.

WINGTIP SPAN: 0.8–1.0 in. (2.0–2.5 cm)

Silvery Blue

Glaucopsyche lygdamus

A relatively recent addition to our butterfly fauna, the Silvery Blue began to appear in our area around 1986, when capture records confirmed it in the Whitefield area. As it has long been common in eastern Canada and northern Maine, it presumably has worked its way into our area from the north. It may easily be mistaken for the Spring Azure but usually prefers more open fields and meadows. It has a more rapid, direct flight, and the silvery-blue luster to its wings makes it more conspicuous. The males are shiny blue above with narrow black margins, and the females have wide, dark borders, and nearly all are dark bluish-brown above. The underside is brownish-gray with small black spots ringed with white. An avid flower visitor; purple vetch, also the larval host, is one of its favorites. Locally, it flies from about mid-May to late June.

HABITAT: Open lowland and upland fields and meadows.

LARVAL HOST: Vetch, white sweet clover, everlasting peas, and others. One brood; probably overwinters as pupa.

WINGTIP SPAN: 0.9–1.2 in. (2.3–3.0 cm)

Swamps and
Wetlands

Brush-Footed Butterflies

Family Nymphalidae

The largest family of true butterflies gets its common name from the reduced size of the front legs of both sexes, and they are often hairy, or brushlike. This family includes many common and well-known groups, such as the fritillaries, admirals, checkerspots, angle wings, and many others. All are primarily flower visitors and are highly conspicuous during the summer months in fields, meadows, and along roadsides. Many are also attracted to damp spots in roadways, and a few are partial to wetlands. Some species, like those of the checkerspots, overwinter as young larvae; others, like the angle wings *(Polygonia),* overwinter as adults and resume flying in early spring. The larvae feed on a wide variety of trees, shrubs, and other plants, and the caterpillars of most species have branching spines.

Question Mark

Polygonia interrogationis

This, as well as the following five species, are popularly called the "angle wings" because of their irregular wing margins. Fresh adults emerge about midsummer and fly well into late summer and early fall, overwintering as adults; worn individuals can be often seen in early spring. The wings of all species are a warm orange-brown above with deeper-brown patterns near the margins and irregular black spots. Their distinctive underside colors and patterns are mottled and streaked with shades of brown and gray. These cryptic patterns give them a "dead leaf" appearance at rest (with wings folded over their backs). These underside patterns enable students to separate the species. Each species has a metallic stigma on the hind wings beneath in the form of a "comma," or, for this species, a "question mark." All are flower visitors but are just as often seen at damp spots along roadways or sipping fermented sap or overripe fruit.

The Question Mark is the largest species, often seen in home gardens, towns, and villages as well as in the country. It is double brooded, and adults may be of the typical spring or winter form, with lightly marked hind wings above, or the summer form, with the hind wings heavily shaded with black. All the angle wings are fast, elusive flyers.

HABITAT: Roadsides, gardens, and open urban clearings.

LARVAL HOST: Hops, elm, nettle. Two broods; overwinters as adult.

WINGTIP SPAN: 2.1–2.6 in. (5.3–6.6 cm)

Eastern Comma

Polygonia comma

Similar to the Question Mark, but smaller, and the underside stigma is in the form of a metallic "comma" against a background of mottled brown shades. Like the Question Mark, the Eastern Comma has two color phases: One has lightly marked hind wings above; the other has much black coloration. Adults are likely to be seen out of hibernation in very early spring and newly hatched ones from late June to late August.

HABITAT: Roadways with damp spots, clearings, and around residential homes and gardens.

LARVAL HOST: Hops, elm, nettle. Unlike that of the Question Mark, the spiny larva of the Eastern Comma usually rests concealed within a loose leaf nest. Two broods; overwinters as adult.

WINGTIP SPAN: 1.7–1.9 in. (4.3–4.8 cm)

Satyr Comma

Polygonia satyrus

The Satyr Comma is the only native member of the genus that is quite rare in northern New Hampshire, as it is generally more northern in distribution; it is more common in northern forested regions in Maine and eastern Canada. James P. Holmes, of Jefferson, took a specimen of it in New Hampshire, along the Scott's Bog Road north of the Second Connecticut Lake. Jim doubtless has fond memories of this capture, even though I had the brief honor of recognizing the specimen as an unusually marked angle wing and tried for it at first while walking ahead of him along the roadway. The frustration of my failed attempt was followed by a shout of jubilation from Jim as he netted the specimen with a spectacular backup shot. Being bested by a butterfly is an acceptable defeat, but the sting of being outclassed by one's collecting companion lingers.

The Satyr is very similar to the other angle wings in color and pattern and can be identified only by someone familiar with the species. It is also much like the others in habits and flies at about the same time: most of July and into August.

HABITAT: Along roadways and in clearings through northern boreal forested regions.

LARVAL HOST: Most likely currant or gooseberry *(Ribes)*. One brood; overwinters as adult.

WINGTIP SPAN: 1.7–1.9 in. (4.3–4.8 cm)

Green Comma

Polygonia faunus

Probably our most common angle wing, the Green Comma is likely to be seen along any roadway through wooded areas and frequently in open clearings, visiting flowers. As indicated by its common name, the cryptically mottled pattern of the underside has flecks of green coloration near the margins. During July and early August, a drive up the Jefferson Notch Road is sure to reveal numbers of this species sipping mud from roadside damp spots and visiting flowers like joe-pye weed, pearly everlasting, and aster. Like the other angle wings, it is a swift and elusive flyer when alarmed.

HABITAT: Forests and woodlands, especially along roadways through these areas.

LARVAL HOST: Birch, willow, alder, currant, and gooseberry. One brood; overwinters as adult.

WINGTIP SPAN: 1.7–1.9 in. (4.3–4.8 cm)

Hoary Comma

Polygonia gracilis

Although Donald Lennox has a capture record of this species in or near Jefferson, I have never found it much farther south than the Colebrook (Diamond Pond) area. It is usually quite common in the Connecticut Lakes Region along the logging roads, especially along the road to Scott's Bog, north of the Second Lake. Underneath, the pattern is quite distinctive and fairly easy to separate from the other species on sight: The outer portion of the lower wing surfaces is dusted and frosted with extensive white coloration. It has a somewhat less vigorous flight than the others and is fond of many roadside flowers as well as damp patches of roadway. It usually reaches peak abundance from early to mid-August.

HABITAT: Canadian-zone woodlands and along logging roads in the extreme northern part of the state.

LARVAL HOST: Currant and gooseberry. One brood; overwinters as adult.

WINGTIP SPAN: 1.4–1.6 in. (3.6–4.1 cm)

Gray Comma

Polygonia progne

Though often seen in wooded clearings, the Gray Comma seems to prefer a bit more open environment. It is often found in open fields, as well as along paths and roadways, visiting flowers and damp spots. The underside colors are a more uniform gray with fine black streaks. Above, it is similar to all the others and flies at about the same time.

HABITAT: Open roadways in forested areas and near open fields; a common species likely to be seen alongside the railroad beds into Big Cherry Pond or along the Hazen Road near the Whitefield airport.

LARVAL HOST: Birch, currant, gooseberry. One brood; overwinters as adult.

WINGTIP SPAN: 1.6–1.8 in. (4.1–4.6 cm)

Compton Tortoiseshell

Nymphalis vaualbum

A large, beautifully marked butterfly, deep brownish-orange above with a distinctive pattern of large black patches and spots. It is closely related to the angle wings but is much larger. Like most angle wings, the underside is a cryptic pattern of gray-brown streaks and mottling. It is an extremely fast and elusive flyer and is often seen perching at damp spots along roadways and, occasionally, visiting flowers. It favors wooded and forested country and, although not really common in northern New Hampshire, it appears regularly each season. In Pennsylvania and the Adirondack Mountains, it is abundant in some places. Here in the White Mountains, open roadways and logging roads through mixed woodlands are likely places to see it, and I have found it along the Jefferson Notch Road. It is also sometimes seen on high mountain trails, frequently above tree line. Often in late fall this species is seen flying about the eaves of houses and outbuildings, presumably looking for a place to overwinter.

HABITAT: Well-lit roadways and clearings through high- and low-elevation forest.

LARVAL HOST: Northern white birch, willow, and, perhaps, poplar. The spiny larvae feed socially. One brood; overwinters as adult.

WINGTIP SPAN: 2.5–2.7 in. (6.4–6.9 cm)

Mourning Cloak

Nymphalis antiopa

The Mourning Cloak is familiar to nearly everyone, with its very dark, yellow-bordered wings. It is quite different from the Compton Tortoiseshell yet, actually, very closely related to it. It is a common sight in the first warm days of spring, when overwintered adults emerge from hibernation, and even more abundant when their progeny hatch from chrysalides, or pupae, in mid- to late summer. Its flight is not as fast or elusive as that of the Compton Tortoiseshell, but, like that species, it seems to prefer sipping mud along damp roadways as much as visiting flowers. The larvae of the Mourning Cloak are also gregarious when young but tend to become solitary feeders in the last larval stage. The caterpillars are spiny and blackish in color, with a row of deep-red dorsal spots on each segment. This butterfly is apparently less common in Europe; in England it is known as the Camberwell Beauty.

HABITAT: Clearings and roadways near wooded areas.

LARVAL HOST: Willow, elm, poplar, hackberry. Two broods; overwinters as adult.

WINGTIP SPAN: 2.8–3.3 in. (7.1–8.4 cm)

Milbert's Tortoiseshell

Nymphalis milberti

Much smaller in size than the Compton Tortoiseshell and the Mourning Cloak, Milbert's Tortoiseshell is nonetheless a colorful member of this group, with wings above a deep brownish-black near the base with two red bars near the front-edge portion of the forewing and wide orange bands, edged with yellow, near the margins. Like the others the underside is cryptically colored to resemble a dead leaf. It has a fast and elusive flight and is more fond of flowers than many of its relatives are. Although a common lowland species, it is equally common, and frequently more abundant, high up in the alpine zone of our mountains; it is often seen in numbers along the cog railway visiting alpine goldenrod on the Presidential Range. It flies in July and August.

HABITAT: Open fields, meadows, and clearings along roadways.

LARVAL HOST: Nettles. The larvae are brownish and spiny and feed in a colony on the terminal portions of the plant. Two broods; overwinters as adult or pupa.

WINGTIP SPAN: 1.7–1.8 in. (4.3–4.6 cm)

American Lady

Vanessa virginiensis

The colorful patchwork of orange-brown and black on the upper-wing surfaces characterize this species, as well as the next species, the very similar and familiar Painted Lady. Both species have a few white spots near the tips of the forewings. Overwintered adults of *virginiensis* are sometimes seen in spring and newly hatched summer-generation adults from early July into September. Although fairly common, its abundance is subject to periodic fluctuation. It has a fast, elusive flight and visits many kinds of flowers. This species also occurs in Europe.

HABITAT: Open fields, sunny clearings, and roadsides.

LARVAL HOST: Pearly everlasting and related plants. The black-banded, spiny larva rests within a silken nest that is made by fastening together the leaves and flower buds of the host plant. Two broods; overwinters as adult or pupa.

WINGTIP SPAN: 1.7–2.1 in. (4.3–5.3 cm)

Painted Lady

Vanessa cardui

With markings very similar to the American Lady, the Painted Lady is likewise common in parts of Europe and Asia. It is also subject to great population fluctuations; it is common in some years and hardly ever seen in others. During periods of great abundance, it tends to become migratory. It is an avid flower visitor and, during its good years, can be seen in July and August.

HABITAT: Fields and open sunny areas; it is often seen in the alpine zone of the White Mountains as well as in the lowlands.

LARVAL HOST: Various Compositae: thistles, burdock, sunflowers, mallow, hollyhock, and many other cultivated plants. The larva lives in a loose nest of leaves and buds. Two broods; overwinters as adult or pupa.

WINGTIP SPAN: 2.3–2.4 in. (5.8–6.0 cm)

Red Admiral

Vanessa atalanta

This species, with its deep brownish-black upper wings, bold red bands, and white spots, is well-known throughout the world. The underside colors of this species, *virginiensis,* and *cardui* are more diffuse and cryptic. Like some of its relatives, the Red Admiral sometimes builds up huge populations and becomes migratory. One such noteworthy flight occurred in June 1957 here in the Northeast, when great numbers swarmed across Maine and extended as far north as Newfoundland. In average years it is likely to be seen most anytime from spring throughout summer. It visits flowers regularly, as well as sap and fermenting fruit.

HABITAT: Very general and occurs in many environments: fields, roadsides, woodland clearings.

LARVAL HOST: Nettle, hops. Two broods; overwinters as adult and pupa.

WINGTIP SPAN: 2.0–2.3 in. (5.1–5.8 cm)

Great Spangled Fritillary

Speyeria cybele

This and the next two species are generally referred to as the greater fritillaries, or "silverspots." They are conspicuous, fast-flying butterflies, often seen rapidly coursing through fields and meadows during the summer months. All are avid flower visitors and are especially fond of thistle blossoms, milkweed, and dogbane. The upper-wing colors of the three species are warm orange-brown with black spots and scalloped markings. Underneath, the bright silver spotting on the hind wings gives them their popular nickname. The larvae of all our North American *Speyeria* feed on violets and are active only at night. The Great Spangled Fritillary is our largest species and is common in July. In the field our species are sometimes difficult to distinguish; however, when at rest on flowers, the underside pattern of spots has a distinctive look; with a little study and observation, the eye can be trained to recognize them pretty reliably. One species, *aphrodite,* generally flies later than the other two.

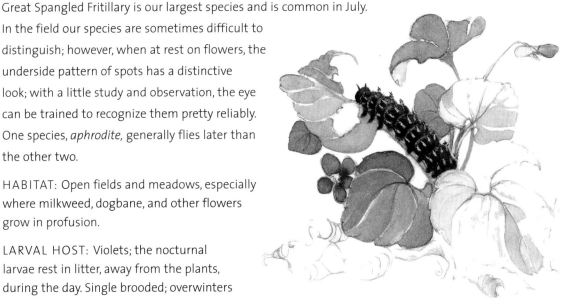

HABITAT: Open fields and meadows, especially where milkweed, dogbane, and other flowers grow in profusion.

LARVAL HOST: Violets; the nocturnal larvae rest in litter, away from the plants, during the day. Single brooded; overwinters as a young larva.

WINGTIP SPAN: 2.3–2.8 in. (5.8–7.1 cm)

Aphrodite

Speyeria aphrodite

Smaller than our other two species, the Aphrodite is usually a brighter orange-brown above and flies somewhat later, from late July often into September. It is more likely to favor open spaces and sometimes strays into the alpine zone of our high mountains.

HABITAT: Open fields and meadows, sunny edges of roadsides.

LARVAL HOST: Violets. One brood; overwinters as a young larva.

WINGTIP SPAN: 2.1–2.4 in. (5.3–6.1 cm)

Atlantis Fritillary

Speyeria atlantis

The Atlantis, our most common fritillary, is more of a reddish-brown above and begins flying a bit earlier than *cybele* and *aphrodite*, flying from about mid-June until late July and often into August. Although preferring open spaces, *atlantis* is more tolerant of shaded areas and is often seen in sheltered woodland clearings as well as in fields and along roadsides.

HABITAT: Same as that of *aphrodite*, as noted previously.

LARVAL HOST: Violets. One brood; overwinters as a young larva.

WINGTIP SPAN: 2.3–2.4 in. (5.8–6.1 cm)

Bog Fritillary

Boloria eunomia

One of the smaller or "lesser" fritillaries, *eunomia* is a true bog endemic, limited to fairly open sphagnum bogs. It has a typical fritillary color and pattern above, with dull silver spotting beneath. The Bog Fritillary is more of a northern species, and its occurrence in New Hampshire is speculative. There is an active colony of it in extreme western Maine, very near the New Hampshire state line, and I have taken it in a large, open bog on the Maine side above Errol, New Hampshire. This particular bog extends into New Hampshire, as do a number of similar habitats along the Magalloway River, and it seems very likely that small colonies of this butterfly could occur in the extreme northeastern portion of New Hampshire and other remote areas. It has an extremely brief flight period, just a matter of a few days, in mid-June. The flight is rapid and direct, usually close to the ground. It will often rest with wings expanded on the foliage of bog heaths or black spruce, visiting flowers occasionally.

HABITAT: Limited to bogs, as noted above.

LARVAL HOST: Perhaps willow violets, or *Vaccinium*. One brood. Overwhites as late-stage larva.

WINGTIP SPAN: 1.5 in. (3.8 cm)

Silver-bordered Fritillary

Boloria selene

Another of our small fritillaries, the Silver-bordered Fritillary, general in distribution and quite common, appears in late spring, flying from early June into early July. The summer brood, equally common, appears in August. Like the greater fritillaries the underside of the hind wing has an abundance of silver spots. Common in fields and moist meadows, it visits many kinds of flowers.

HABITAT: Open fields, moist meadows, and roadside clearings.

LARVAL HOST: Probably violets. Two broods; overwinters as a newly hatched or half-grown larva.

WINGTIP SPAN: 1.4 in. (3.6 cm)

Meadow Fritillary

Boloria bellona

Although generally common in many parts of the East, the Meadow Fritillary is quite rare in northern New Hampshire for reasons that are unclear. It seems to be highly sporadic, showing up in small numbers over very long periods of time. I have a single capture record of it from Lancaster on 24 August 1957 and haven't seen it locally since. It is a butterfly of open, moist meadows or partially grown-in old fields and does not appear to be habitat-restricted in any way. I found numbers of them in June 1971, flying through a roadside meadow in Oxford County, Maine, near the New Hampshire state line, but as this spot is now grown in with trees, one would not expect to see them there again. Like all the lesser fritillaries, the wings above have a typical orange-brown black spotted pattern. The underside of the hind wing, however, lacks silver spots; it's a mute pattern of orange-brown and grayish-purple bands.

HABITAT: Moist, open meadows and old fields.

LARVAL HOST: Violets. Probably double brooded in our area. Overwinters as late-stage larva.

WINGTIP SPAN: 1.6–1.8 in. (4.1–4.6 cm)

White Mountain Fritillary

Boloria chariclea montina

Certainly one of our most famous and noteworthy butterflies, *montina,* described by S. H. Scudder in 1863, is a unique and geographically isolated subspecies, occurring only on New Hampshire's Presidential Range above an elevation of 4,000 feet. The species *chariclea* flies in mountainous portions of Europe and North America and has a number of distinct subspecies in parts of the American West and Canada. It is slightly smaller than the Meadow Fritillary but very similar in color and pattern. As with most alpine insects, it is active only during periods of warm sunshine. The flight period begins as early as late July, with peak flights occurring the first two weeks of August, depending on the season. It is fond of flowers, alpine goldenrod being a favorite.

HABITAT: Lush, moist areas near sheltered spots, and wet springs around rocky outcroppings at an elevation of about 4,500 feet. The Cragway Spring area on the Mount Washington Auto Road is a particularly good spot to see it.

LARVAL HOST: Not known for certain, possibly blueberry or willow. Single brooded; overwinters as first-stage larva.

WINGTIP SPAN: 1.4–1.6 in. (3.6–4.1 cm)

Pearl Crescent

Phyciodes tharos

Crescents are small butterflies, usually with patchwork patterns of orange-brown, black, and yellowish coloration. Underneath, a small crescent-shaped mark near the rear portion of the hind wing gives these butterflies their popular name. Our species, sometimes referred to as the Northern Pearl Crescent, is a very early summer species that one is likely to notice in numbers along dirt roads, where they often congregate at damp spots or puddles. Authors of some of the more recent butterfly books consider our northern populations to represent a distinct species; if so, it is very close to the common eastern *tharos* in appearance and behavior and shares a similar habitat. It is not a strong flyer and stays close to the ground unless alarmed, when it can move quickly. It often exhibits territorial behavior. It is most often seen from mid-June to mid-July and is a frequent flower visitor.

HABITAT: Fields, meadows, and especially damp spots along dirt roads, where numbers can usually be seen.

LARVAL HOST: Asters. Double brooded throughout much of its northern range, but my capture records indicate that it may be single brooded in our area. Overwinters as partly grown larva.

WINGTIP SPAN: 1.3–1.5 in. (3.3–3.8 cm)

Tawny Crescent

Phyciodes batesii

There is some debate as to whether or not this species occurs in New Hampshire at the present time. I have never seen nor taken it, although, according to William Fiske, Dr. S. H. Scudder apparently took it in the White Mountains on 7 June, many years ago. It is so much like the common Pearl Crescent on the upper surface of the wings that it may easily be overlooked. The heavier pattern of black markings on the upper-wing surfaces, however, give *batesii* a darker appearance when the two are compared, and there are differences in the lower surface of the hind wings. If it does occur within the northern part of the state, it would likely be localized in small colonies. Adults would be expected in June.

HABITAT: Much the same as for the Pearl Crescent.

LARVAL HOST: Blue wood aster *(Aster undulatus)*. One brood. Overwinters as partly grown larva.

WINGTIP SPAN: 1.3–1.5 in. (3.3–3.8 cm)

Silvery Checkerspot

Chlosyne nycteis

Although similar to the crescents, the checkerspots are larger in size and have slightly different markings. Their popular name derives from the pale, dark-bordered spotting against a tawny or reddish background on the underside of the hind wing in a checkered effect. In *An Annotated Catalog of the Butterflies of New Hampshire* (1901), William F. Fiske reported collecting the Silvery Checkerspot in the Pinkham Notch area near the Glen House. I have never seen nor taken it in New Hampshire, in spite of many searches through this area, and I suspect that the old colonies of this butterfly have long since disappeared. Late June and early July would be the time to expect it.

HABITAT: Open meadows, lakeshores, and roadsides.

LARVAL HOST: Asters, sunflowers. One brood; overwinters as a partly grown larva.

WINGTIP SPAN: 1.5–1.6 in. (3.8–4.1 cm)

Harris's Checkerspot

Chlosyne harrisii

Harris's Checkerspot is abundant in the White Mountain region and is similar to the Silvery, but the strong checkered pattern on the underside of the hind wing is more pronounced. Adults fly from late June into July and are fond of many kinds of flowers, but freshly hatched adults are also likely to be seen in numbers at damp spots and puddles along dirt roads, often flying with the Pearl Crescent and other early-summer species. The spiny orange-and-black larva of this species is also a common sight during late spring and is often seen in considerable numbers on young plants of the northern white aster, the larval host. The eggs are laid on this plant during midsummer, and the young larvae feed as a colony within a web near the flowers on the upper part of the stalk. The larvae overwinter, probably under deep snow and litter, close to the ground. In spring they emerge to resume feeding singly or in small groups of two or three.

HABITAT: Moist meadows and fields, where they tend to be somewhat local.

LARVAL HOST: Northern white aster *(Aster umbellatus)*. One brood; overwinters as partly grown larva.

WINGTIP SPAN: 1.4–1.7 in. (3.6–4.3 cm)

Baltimore

Euphydryas phaeton

This handsome, strikingly marked butterfly is well-known throughout the Northeast and occurs in extremely local colonies near damp meadows and swampy areas where turtlehead (the primary larval host) grows. The adult colors are unmistakable: black upper wings with marginal rows of yellowish-white spots and bright-red spotting along the borders. The underside colors are similar, with heavy checkering of the red and light colors. It is an avid flower visitor but never strays far from its swampy habitat. Like the other checkerspots, after hatching, the young larvae live in a colony on the turtlehead plants for the remainder of the summer. Adults fly from mid-June to the first part of July the following year. The abundance of this species appears to be directly linked to that of the host plant. In the early 1970s at a swampy roadside area near Stewartstown where turtlehead thrived, I observed hundreds of Baltimore larvae late one spring. I returned in 1995—the wet meadow was just as I remembered it, except that turtlehead apparently no longer grows there. As I expected, I saw no signs of the butterfly.

HABITAT: Wet meadows or swamps with turtlehead, with butterflies often found along roadsides near these areas.

LARVAL HOST: Turtlehead, for the young first-summer larvae, then transitioning to ash or honeysuckle or continuing to feed on turtlehead. One brood, overwinters as young larva.

WINGTIP SPAN: 1.8–1.9 in. (4.6–4.8 cm)

White Admiral

Limenitis arthemis arthemis

A conspicuous and easily recognized butterfly with deep blue-black wings and broad white bands on upper and lower surfaces. Although generally distributed, the White Admiral is usually more numerous near wet areas or along dirt roadways bordering brooks or small streams, where great numbers are often seen visiting damp spots or animal droppings. It frequently also visits flowers in open meadows and fields near these areas, flying from mid-June into July and again in August. The White Admiral is the more northern expression of a complex of closely related color forms. In southern New England this butterfly tends to be replaced by the Red-spotted Purple, which lacks the white bands and has more pronounced red spotting on the wings beneath. This color form was once considered to be a distinct species, but research has shown that in areas where the two forms overlap, much hybridization takes place, often producing partially white-banded individuals. All the species of this genus, including the Viceroy, are very closely related genetically, and occasional hybrids occur between a number of these other species throughout North America where their ranges overlap.

HABITAT: Dirt roads, trails, and clearings, especially near wet areas, brooks, or small streams.

LARVAL HOST: Yellow birch, willow, poplar. Two broods; young larvae overwinter in a shelter, or hibernaculum, upon the food plant.

WINGTIP SPAN: 2.3–2.6 in. (5.8–6.6 cm)

Viceroy

Limenitis archippus

Although a close relative of the White Admiral, the common and widespread Viceroy looks nothing like its white-banded next of kin but instead is an almost perfect duplicate of the larger Monarch, a butterfly of an entirely different family. So closely are the familiar Monarch's orange and black colors copied by the Viceroy that about the only clues to separating them in the field are the Viceroy's considerably smaller size and different flight characteristics. This manner of copying, or mimicking, another species is often used as an example of Batesian mimicry: A species presumably gains protection by duplicating the color and pattern of another species that has a strong natural defense against predators, such as poisonous or distasteful body substances, as in the case of the Monarch. Birds and other predators learn to avoid the Monarch as a food target; thinking that the Viceroy is another Monarch, they will leave it alone, even though it is a perfectly suitable food source.

The Viceroy's close relationship with the White Admiral becomes evident in a comparison of structure, breeding habits, and larva characteristics. The caterpillars of both species are nearly identical, and they utilize similar host plants. The very young larva of the Viceroy also overwinters within a rolled portion of the tip of the food leaf (hibernaculum), emerging to resume feeding as the leaf buds open in spring. As stated previously, members of this genus form a close association of species that can produce hybrids, although these are quite rare in nature. One such interesting individual was captured a few years ago, near Big Cherry Pond, by Dr. Donald H. Miller of Lyndon State College. This unusual specimen had the dark markings of the White Admiral but had a dark-lined orange flush on its wings, which is good circumstantial evidence of hybridization with the Viceroy. The Viceroy is common throughout summer, from mid-June through August, and is fond of many kinds of flowers.

HABITAT: Open fields and damp meadows, especially fields with an abundance of willow saplings.

LARVAL HOST: Willows, poplars, cherry, and several others. Two broods; overwinters as young larva.

WINGTIP SPAN: 2.6–2.8 in. (6.6–7.1 cm)

Alpine Zone

Satyrs and Wood Nymphs

Family Nymphalidae

These are medium-sized butterflies, usually with uniform dark-brown coloration above and a streaked, mottled pattern beneath, which gives them a very dark, somber appearance. Nearly all species have a characteristic pattern of black "eyespot" markings near the upper- and lower-wing margins, giving rise to popular nicknames such as "goggle-eye," "pearly-eyed brown," and the like. They are generally butterflies of shaded habitats or sheltered margins of woodlands, although a few are better known as meadow or open-field species. Because they often fly with an elusive, erratic, bouncy flight, those species that prefer shade or woodland margins are thus able to give a predator (or a determined butterfly collector) a real challenge. The larvae feed on a variety of grasses and sedges. Two species of the genus *Oeneis* are well known as true arctic butterflies and typically are found in arctic or tundra habitats in Labrador or the high arctic barrens of North America. One of these, the White Mountain Butterfly, is perhaps New Hampshire's most famous butterfly, with a relict colony occurring in the high alpine zone of the Presidential Range. The other, the Jutta Arctic, is a true bog endemic. Another species, the Common Ringlet, is a relatively recent addition to our butterfly fauna, preferring open fields and meadows and having a lighter brownish-ocher coloration.

Northern Pearly Eye

Enodia anthedon

Our Northern Pearly Eye is now known to be distinct from the more southern species, *Enodia portlandia,* which is common and widespread throughout most of the eastern United States, although superficially the two are very similar. The Northern Pearly Eye is a medium-sized brown butterfly that is most often seen along dirt roads near swampy thickets that have plenty of tall grasses and sedges. In these habitats the males can be seen congregating at mud puddles and damp spots during the early part of the flight season, sometimes in great numbers. Butterflies of this genus also have a tendency to be crepuscular, as they are active at dusk, and an early evening drive along the old roadway past the Whitefield airport hangars from early to mid-July is sure to reveal numbers of this species gathered at damp spots. They have an erratic, dodging flight; when disturbed, they will often fly erratically in circles, settle on sedges or alder foliage, and frequently will return to the same spot on the roadway.

HABITAT: Grassy clearings and thickets near swampy woods.

LARVAL HOST: Grasses. One brood; overwinters as a partly grown larva.

WINGTIP SPAN: 2.0 in. (5.1 cm)

Eyed Brown

Satyrodes eurydice

Similar to the Pearly Eye but smaller, with a lighter yellow-brown color and slightly different markings. Like most other species in this family, the Eyed Brown has a marginal row of black eyespot markings on upper- and lower-wing surfaces. It often flies in the same kind of habitat as the Pearly Eye, and the two species are often seen together, though the Eyed Brown tends to favor more open sedge meadows and fields. It is very common from late June to late July. A very close but distinct species, the Appalachian Brown *(Satyrodes appalachia),* occurs marginally in southern New Hampshire and southward. It is slightly larger, a somewhat different shade of brown, and has a distinct habitat difference, preferring shaded swampy woods and bottomlands. A brief discussion of this latter species is included in Appendix A.

HABITAT: Associated with swampy, open sedge meadows; the flight is low and erratic through sedge clumps or hummocks.

LARVAL HOST: Sedges. One brood; overwinters as a partly grown larva.

WINGTIP SPAN: 1.5–1.9 in. (3.8–4.8 cm)

Little Wood Satyr

Megisto cymela

Slightly smaller than the Eyed Brown and a darker grayish-brown color, the Little Wood Satyr is much more restricted to shaded thickets and edges of open woods; when alarmed, it can effectively dodge into the shaded seclusion of the forest. It flies from early June to early July. The flight is erratic and elusive.

HABITAT: Open deciduous woods or in wooded margins of wet meadows with brush or shrubby growth.

LARVAL HOST: Grasses. One brood; overwinters as a partly grown larva.

WINGTIP SPAN: 1.4–1.5 in. (3.6–3.8 cm)

Common Ringlet

Coenonympha tullia

During the early 1970s the Common Ringlet began expanding its range from Ontario and western Quebec into New England. Well-known butterfly authority Dr. Clifford D. Ferris captured a specimen of it in central Maine in 1969, and in June 1970, I captured two females near Groveton. At the same time two other New Hampshire collectors began seeing it along the Connecticut River Valley, where it appeared to have moved eastward from earlier colonies discovered in New York state. A year or so later, it had become well established in northern Vermont, and increased captures and sightings in New Hampshire and other New England states indicated that it was spreading rapidly. It is our smallest satyr, a warm brownish-ocher color with faint black dots for eyespot markings, which are completely lacking on some individual specimens. The underside of the hind wing is a greenish-gray with marbled light shades. It favors open, grassy fields and is now perhaps our most abundant butterfly.

The Common Ringlet has infiltrated nearly every open environment, and there seems to be no limit to its range potential here in the Northeast. Speculation on this varies, but a consensus favors the idea that, like many riparian, or grass-feeding species, recent expansion of cleared land for interstate highways, leaving wide, grassy margins, offers avenues with a virtually unlimited food supply through which these species can spread and become established.

HABITAT: Virtually everywhere now, favoring open, grassy fields and clearings.

LARVAL HOST: Grasses. Two broods; probably overwinters as a young larva.

WINGTIP SPAN: 1.2–1.8 in (3.0–4.6 cm)

Common Wood Nymph

Cercyonis pegala

Commonly seen in July and early August, this medium-large butterfly is often flushed from the grasses and goldenrod of maturing fields and meadows, as well as from wooded thickets. It appears to be all black but is actually a very dark brown. Two prominent black eyespots adorn the forewings near the margins, and in more southern and coastal parts of its range, these spots tend to be ringed with a yellow aura or are enclosed in a large yellow patch. Our northern form, however, almost always lacks this yellow shading, and the butterfly appears unicolorous. Like most satyrs, it has a dodging, erratic flight and frequently visits flowers.

HABITAT: Edges of woods and thickets but, just as often, open fields and meadows.

LARVAL HOST: Grasses. One brood; overwinters as a newly hatched larva.

WINGTIP SPAN: 1.9–2.0 in. (4.8–5.1 cm)

Jutta Arctic

Oeneis jutta

This and the next species belong to a genus of truly arctic butterflies that inhabit the tundra and boggy taiga life zones of the coldest regions on Earth. The Jutta Arctic is a brownish butterfly that occurs in scattered colonies in northern New England as a strict bog endemic. Its unique habitat requirements are such that it does not occur in every bog, but only those with a substantial growth of stunted black spruce, usually at the bog rims or margins. A walk through a tangle of gaunt saplings will often flush this species from its perch on a small dead spruce limb or trunk, when it will fly in a dazzlingly erratic and elusive pattern through a clearing and settle on another such perch, usually close to the ground, and seem to disappear. The underside wing colors are cryptically mottled and streaked with gray and brown coloration, giving them ample protection against the background of peeling, mossy bark on which they settle. A number of small black eyespots adorn the outer portions of the wings of both sexes, and, in the females, the spots are often surrounded by an aura of yellow. They occasionally will visit flowers; the white blossoms of Labrador tea, a common bog shrub, are a

favorite nectar source. A small, sheltered bog just off the Bray Hill Road between Jefferson and Whitefield had an active colony of this species for many years. Just as it looked as though it might have died out, I saw a single adult there in June 1995; I'm hoping it will make a comeback. A number of the Jutta Arctic were also recently observed in the boggy margins of Little Cherry Pond, and at least one adult was noted in nearby Mud Pond Bog. Like the Bog Copper there is some indication that the Jutta Arctic is capable of straying occasionally and locating other suitable bog habitats to colonize. On a recent trip to Oxford County, Maine, I was hiking through mixed hardwood and spruce forest, between two bog habitats, and I was surprised to find a Jutta there, clearly out of its element and presumably on the move. In Maine the Jutta Arctic begins flying in late May, but it flies a little later here in the White Mountains, from about the first week of June until the middle of the month.

HABITAT: Sphagnum, black-spruce bogs.

LARVAL HOST: A bog sedge (*Carex trisperma billingsii*). Donald Lennox is one of the few people to have ever reared the Jutta, and the University of New Hampshire herbarium provided the plant identification. Single brooded; the partly grown larva overwinters.

WINGTIP SPAN: 1.8–1.9 in. (4.6–4.8 cm)

White Mountain Butterfly

Oeneis melissa semidea

There is perhaps no more famous denizen of the Presidential Range alpine zone than this butterfly. Described by naturalist Thomas Say in 1828, this species has drawn the attention and curiosity of countless scientists, researchers, and amateur naturalists for many years. Its unique behavior and habitat set it apart from nearly all other butterflies, and its adaptations to exist and thrive in one of the most bleak and inhospitable environments on the continent make it one of the true marvels of nature. Like a number of other insects, the White Mountain Butterfly represents an isolated mountain population of a species more typical and widespread in the tundra regions of the North American Arctic. Over the ages subtle changes in its behavior, color, and pattern have produced distinct differences from its northern relatives, resulting in a unique geographic subspecies. A similar situation has taken place with *melissa* in the high portions of the Rocky Mountains, from Colorado and Montana northward into British Columbia, and low-elevation colonies of it occur in Labrador. An abundance of hiking trails on the Presidential Range afford the observer ample opportunity to see this butterfly, which is on the wing from the end of June through the first two or three weeks in July at elevations between 5,000 and 5,500 feet. They are commonly flushed along the hiking trails or may be seen flying erratically over the rock-strewn alpine landscape, often

congregating, or "hilltopping," near rocky outcroppings. During the early part of its flight period, the males can be somewhat aggressive and territorial, and squabbling pairs of these brownish butterflies are often seen along the cog railway. When alarmed, it will fly quickly, often carried for some distance by the almost constant wind. Then, just as quickly, it will drop down out of sight, usually alighting on the ground or bare rock. There, it will often move with quick starts, "tilting" its wings to catch the sunlight while, at the same time, minimizing its shadow effect so that its cryptic underside colors blend well with the moss- and lichen-encrusted rocks. Like other mountain insects *semidea* is active only when the sunlight is bright and strong; the appearance of sudden cloud cover and the associated drop in temperature will cause it to disappear as it finds shelter in the rock crevices. The White Mountain Butterfly is most often seen in numbers on the high, grassy "lawns" just below the summit peaks. Bigelow Lawn and the Cow Pasture of Mount Washington and Monticello Lawn on Mount Jefferson are typical environments for it. These gently sloping areas have an abundance of grasses and sedges, and the females will especially favor these portions of the mountains during their egg-laying period.

HABITAT: Limited strictly to the high mountains of the Presidential Range, usually above a 5,000-foot elevation.

LARVAL HOST: Bigelow's Sedge *(Carex bigelowii)*. One brood; overwinters as a young larva.

WINGTIP SPAN: 1.9–1.8 in. (4.8–4.6 cm)

Old Fields

The Monarchs

Family Nymphalidae

The Monarchs belong to the subfamily Danaidae. Although this subfamily is chiefly tropical, with very few species in North America, the well-known and famous Monarch is the only species that occurs throughout our area. The Danaids are mostly large butterflies with a slow, deliberate flight, as though they were aware that they have little to fear from birds and other predators because of their bad-tasting or disagreeable body fluids. The males of our species have a patch of scent scales (androconia) on the hind wings that can be manipulated by hair pencils on the abdomen to disperse their odor. The larvae feed on various milkweeds and nightshades: plants with acrid, milky, poisonous juices that contribute to the butterfly's protective body chemistry.

The Butterflies of the White Mounatins

Monarch

Danaus plexippus

The familiar orange-and-black Monarch hardly needs a description, as its casual, majestic flight over fields and clearings during the summer months is a familiar sight to nearly everyone. Just as familiar, perhaps, is the fleshy yellow-, black-, and white-striped larva, sometimes seen in numbers on milkweed plants. The Monarch, of course, is the famous migrator, with huge continental flights each fall to coastal mountain forests in Mexico. Here in northern New England, we sometimes see large numbers of Monarchs toward the end of summer, often heading south along road and river flyways. It is fond of many wild and cultivated flowers, and the blossoms of its larval host, the common milkweed, are a favorite.

HABITAT: General; all open areas, fields, and clearings.

LARVAL HOST: Various milkweeds. A number of broods occur during the adult's flight northward each season from Mexico. Overwinterings does not occur at any stage; all broods fully mature and migrate as adults.

WINGTIP SPAN: 3.5–3.9 in. (8.9–9.9 cm)

Appendix A

Accidental, Casual, and Stray Species and Unusual Records

Some of the species listed below are the result of the entrance of migratory species into our area. For some insects this happens quite regularly; for others, their occurrence here is an extremely rare event. Some transient species might become temporary residents, if conditions are favorable, for a season or two of breeding, only to later disappear, unable to withstand the average normal climate and environment. As with any list of unusual records, identifications can sometimes be difficult. This is not a problem with all but one of the species included below; most of these are well known and unmistakable.

Family Papilionidae

PIPEVINE SWALLOWTAIL *(Battus philenor)*
Donald Lennox records either a capture or sight record of this species "5 June 1932, on rhodora, in Jefferson." The northern limit of this very dark greenish-blue swallowtail is probably southern New England. The larva feeds on pipevine *(Aristolochia)*, a common ornamental vine grown around many houses locally. It's quite possible that eggs or larvae of this species could be introduced on plants brought to nurseries from outside our region; these produce a few adults that survive for a while.

SPICEBUSH SWALLOWTAIL *(Papilio troilus)*
Another dark swallowtail that may be resident to southern New Hampshire was collected in Jefferson by a young neighbor of Mr. Lennox in the 1960s. The larva feeds on spicebush, sassafras, sweet bay, and prickly ash. Because it's highly unlikely that any of these plants could grow in our region, this record is probably the result of an accidental introduction.

Family Pieridae

LITTLE YELLOW *(Eurema lisa)*

The Little Yellow, common in tropical America and throughout the southeastern United States, is noted for its migratory habits and frequently enters the New England region along the seacoast, where flights sometimes stray far out over the ocean or a considerable distance inland. Many years ago Donald Lennox caught a straggler of this species near the summit of Mount Adams, on the Presidential Range, at an altitude of more than 5,000 feet, of all places. This species often migrates as far as coastal Massachusetts and Maine, usually in fall.

Family Nymphalidae

AMERICAN SNOUT *(Libytheana carinenta)*

This peculiar little butterfly, with angular wings of light- and dark-brownish coloration and protruding palps on the head forming an elongate, beaklike "snout," is a native of lower Austral and Sonoran life zones. It does, however, have regular migrations, and although it frequently gets into New England, records of it this far north would be extremely rare. Fiske, however, cites two captures of *carinenta* by Dr. F. F. Hodgeman, of Littleton, many years ago (no dates of capture given), apparently along a woods road near Littleton. There are also specimens of it in the University of New Hampshire Insect and Arachnid Collections from Norwich, Vermont, according to Fiske.

VARIEGATED FRITILLARY *(Euptoieta claudia)*

Similar to our larger fritillaries, but lacking silver spots, this species is also known for migrating and straying great distances from its normal southeastern United States range. A few years ago, James P. Holmes, of Jefferson, captured a specimen of it on the Turnpike Road between Jefferson and Riverton. It occasionally gets into southern New England; I have taken it as far north as Massachusetts.

APPALACHIAN BROWN *(Satyrodes appalachia)*

Once thought to be a subspecies of our common Eyed Brown (see page 157), this more southern form, which is a bit larger and darker, is now known to be a distinct species, based on a detailed study of color, structure, and habitat. Our common Eyed Brown occurs in more open sedge meadows, whereas *appalachia* prefers swampy, wooded bottomlands. In a study of *appalachia* by Carde, Shapiro, and Clench (*Psyche,* Vol. 77, No. 1, 1970), the authors cite two northern New Hampshire records for this species, and one locality given is for Jefferson. I am somewhat skeptical of these records because the two species could be confused easily, but I will keep an open mind. One of the specimens is in the American Museum of Natural History, in New York; the other, in the Carnegie Museum of Natural History, in Pittsburgh, and it would be interesting to have these records confirmed. Dr. Donald Miller has a number of capture records of *appalachia* from Hillsborough County, New Hampshire, and it is common in eastern Massachusetts. Quite possibly, some wooded bottomland here in the White Mountains could harbor a colony of this species.

Appendix B

Recommended References

Listed below are a few of the available reference works on butterflies that will assist the student, whether collector or observer. Needless to say, additional field guides on flowers, trees, and shrubs become invaluable to any amateur naturalist, especially to those interested in butterflies or other insects.

Glassberg, Jeffrey. 1999. *Butterflies through Binoculars*. New York: Oxford University Press.
   A very popular, easy-to-use field guide.

Klots, A. B. 1951. *A Field Guide to the Butterflies of North America East of the Great Plains.* Boston: Houghton Mifflin Co.
   This has been the standard eastern reference for decades and, although now a bit out of date, is still in wide use for detailed information not found in many more modern field guides.

Opler, F. A., and G. C. Krizek. 1984. *Butterflies East of the Great Plains: An Illustrated Natural History.* Baltimore: Johns Hopkins University Press.
   Along with a detailed account of eastern species, this magnificent volume contains 324 color photos of butterflies in their natural poses and habitats.

Opler, P. A., and V. Malikul. 1992. *A Field Guide to Eastern Butterflies*. Boston: Houghton Mifflin Co.
   This modern edition of the Peterson Field Guide Series contains a wealth of additional species, with superb color plates of adults, a selection of Dr. Opler's photographs of butterflies in nature, and a number of excellent photographs of butterfly larvae and pupae. It also features many flowers recommended for use in butterfly gardens.

Pyle, R. M. 1981. *The Audubon Society Field Guide to North American Butterflies.* New York: Chanticleer Press.
   A photographic guide to butterflies in nature and their immature stages; covers many additional western species.

Appendix C

New Hampshire's Rare Butterflies

New Hampshire's rare lepidoptera are tracked by two state agencies in order to assess conservation efforts that may be necessary to ensure the survival of these species. The New Hampshire Department of Fish and Game, Nongame and Endangered Species Program has legal jurisdiction over wildlife species listed in the New Hampshire Endangered Species Conservation Act of 1979 (NH RSA 212-A). As of 1997 only five lepidoptera were protected under this law: Karner Blue butterfly *(Lycaeides melissa samuelis)*, Frosted Elfin butterfly *(Incisalia irus)*, Persius Dusky Wing Skipper *(Erynnis persius persius)*, pine barrens Zanclognatha moth *(Zanclognatha martha)*, and Pine Pinion moth *(Lithophane lepida lepida)*.

The New Hampshire Natural Heritage Inventory, a program housed in the New Hampshire Department of Resources and Economic Development's Division of Forests and Lands, cooperates with the Nongame Program and maintains the state's database of rare species and natural communities in New Hampshire. In addition to the five lepidopteran species listed above, the Natural Heritage Inventory tracks more than 125 other wildlife species that are considered rare or imperiled in New Hampshire.

The information on lepidoptera maintained in the Natural Heritage Inventory database is derived almost exclusively from amateur lepidopterists; in fact, assessments of what is rare in the state and, further, the condition of these species globally, are based on records collected by amateur lepidopterists. Unfortunately, records are patchy and often vague, particularly those from the early part of this century. More information is needed, and you can help.

If you observe or collect a species that is tracked by the state or that you consider to be rare or unusual, please share your information with the Nongame Program or Natural Heritage Inventory. They particularly need the following information:

1. Species name
2. Collection location (a map is essential, detailed written directions are extremely helpful)

3. Habitat description (swamp? meadow? the more details you can provide, the better)
4. Specimen location (photos will help for some species)
5. Collector's/Observer's name, address, telephone number, and E-mail address
6. Date and time observed/collected

Under the New Hampshire Endangered Species Conservation Act, a permit from the New Hampshire Fish and Game Department is required for collection of listed species. The Karner Blue butterfly is so imperiled that any activities relating to it must also be permitted by the U.S. Fish and Wildlife Service. Permits are not required for collection of other lepidoptera species, but collectors are encouraged to exercise good judgment to avoid overcollection. Although most lepidoptera species are locally robust enough to withstand prudent collecting (with the notable exceptions of Karner Blues, Frosted Elfins, and Persius Dusky Wings), overcollecting by unscrupulous collectors could deleteriously impact species with limited ranges, particularly those in alpine areas.

To get more information or to report interesting findings, please contact either of the following state agencies:

New Hampshire Nongame and Endangered Species Program
New Hampshire Department of Fish and Game
2 Hazen Drive, Concord, NH 03301
(603) 271–2462

New Hampshire Natural Heritage Inventory
Department of Resources and Economic Development
P.O. Box 1856 (172 Pembroke Road), Concord, NH 03302–1856
(603) 271–3623

New Hampshire Natural Heritage Inventory

Rare Butterfly List

Scientific Name	Common Name	Global/State Rank		U.S. State Listing Code	Number of Locations
HESPERIIDAE					
Achalarus lyciades	Hoary Edge	G5	SA		0
Anatrytone logan	Delaware Skipper	G5	S3S4		(0) 1
Atrytonopsis hianna	Dusted Skipper	G4G5	S3?		2
Erynnis baptisiae	Wild Indigo Dusky Wing	G5	S1		1
Erynnis brizo brizo	Sleepy Dusky Wing	G5T5	S2		3
Erynnis horatius	Horace's Dusky Wing	G5	SU		1
Erynnis lucilius	Columbine Dusky Wing	G4	SH		4
Erynnis persius persius	Persius Dusky Wing	G4T2T3	S1	E	5
Euphyes bimacula	Two-spotted Skipper	G4	S3S4		0
Hesperia comma laurentina	Laurentian Skipper	G5T5	S?		0
Hesperia metea	Cobweb Skipper	G4G5	S3		5
Poanes massasoit	Mulberry Wing	G4	S1S3		0
Pompeius verna	Little Glassy Wing	G5	SU		0
LYCAENIDAE					
Erora laetus	Early Hairstreak	G4	SU		0
Incisalia eryphon SSP 1	Western Banded Elfin	G5TU	SU		0
Incisalia henrici	Henry's Elfin	G5	S2S3		1
Incisalia irus	Frosted Elfin	G3G4	S1	E	7
Incisalia lanoraieensis	Bog Elfin	G3	SH		1
Incisalia polia	Hoary Elfin	G5	SH		0
Lycaeides melissa samuelis	Karner Blue Butterfly	G5T2	S1	LE E	7

Mitoura grynea	Olive Hairstreak	G5	SH	0
Mitoura hesseli	Hessel's Hairstreak	G3G4	SH	1
Satyrium edwardsii	Edward's Hairstreak	G4	S3	2

NYMPHALIDAE

Asterocampa celtis	Hackberry Butterfly	G5	S2?	1
Asterocampa clyton	The Tawny Emperor	G5	SZB	1
Boloria chariclea montina	White Mountain Fritillary	G5T2	S2	3
Chlosyne nycteis	Silvery Crescentspot	G5	SH	0
Oeneis jutta	Jutta Arctic	G5	S3S4	0
Oeneis melissa semidea	White Mountain Butterfly	G5T2	S2	0
Polygonia gracilis	Hoary Comma	G5	S1	4
Polygonia satyrus	Satyr Angle Wing	G5	SU	0
Satyrodes appalachia	Appalachian Brown	G5	S1?	1
Speyeria atlantis	Atlantis Fritillary	G5	S?	0

PIERIDAE

Pieris napi oleracea	Veined White	G5T4	S3	0

Rank Prefix:
G = Global Rank
S = State Rank
T = Global or State rank for a
    subspecies or variety

Rank Suffix:
1 = Critically imperiled due to
    rarity or vulnerability
2 = Imperiled
3 = Rare/uncommon
4 = Widespread but with cause
    for long-term concern
5 = Widepsread, abundant,
    and secure
H = Occurred historically, not
    known to have been
    extirpated
X = Extirpated
?/U = Not ranked/unknown

Listing Codes:
T = Threatened
E = Endangered

Appendix D

Butterfly Clubs and Organizations

Listed below are a few organizations open to anyone interested in butterflies. Included also are their contact addresses for membership as well as dues information. A few organizations are limited to butterflies specifically; some include moths or other insect orders. A brief description follows the organization address.

Connecticut Butterfly Association, P.O. Box 9004, New Haven, CT 06532. Offers butterfly field observations and other activities; publishes a newsletter.

The Lepidopterists' Society, c/o Ron Leuschner, Assistant Treasurer, 1900 John Street, Manhattan Beach, CA 90266-2608; www.earthlife.net/insects/lepsoc.html. A worldwide organization of amateur and professional lepidopterists; publishes a newsletter and a quarterly journal.

New York Butterfly Club, c/o Don Riepe, 29 West Ninth Road, Broad Channel, NY 11693. More than one hundred members in the New York City area and beyond. Publishes monthly newsletter.

North American Butterfly Association, 4 Delaware Road, Morristown, NJ 07960; www.naba.org. Stresses observation and conservation. This group's founder, Jeffrey Glassberg, is the author of the popular book *Butterflies through Binoculars*. The magazine *American Butterflies* is their publication.

Vermont Entomological Society, 49 Lover's Lane, Grand Isle, VT 05458; www.uvm. edu/~rtbell/VES.html. An organization of amateur and professional naturalists interested in all insect orders, including many members with specific interests in butterflies. Occasional summer field trips and off-season activities, lectures, and the like, are scheduled. *Entoforce* is the published newsletter.

The Xerces Society, 4828 S.E. Hawthorne Boulevard, Portland, OR 97215; 503–232–6639; www.xerces.org. Emphasizes conservation and habitat protection of butterflies, moths, and terrestrial invertebrates. Field trips are planned to include butterfly surveys, counts, and so forth. The title of their publication is *Wings*.

Bibliography

Carde, R. T., A. M. Shapiro, and H. K. Clench. 1970. Sibling Species in the Eurydice Group of Lethe (Lepidoptera, Satyridae). *Psyche* 77(1): 70–103.

Farquhar, D. W. 1934. *The Lepidoptera of New England.* Unpublished thesis, Cambridge, Mass.

Fiske, W. F. 1901. *An Annotated Catalog of the Butterflies of New Hampshire.* Durham: College of Agriculture and the Mechanical Arts (Technical Bulletin, no. 1).

Hagen, R. H., R. C. Lederhouse, J. L. Bossart, and M. J. Scriber. 1991. *Papilio canadensis* and *P. glaucus* (Papillonidae) are Distinct Species. *Jour. Lepid. Soc.* 45(4): 245–58.

Hodges, R. W., et al. 1983. *Check List of the Lepidoptera of America North of Mexico.* E. W. Classey Ltd., & the Wedge Entomological Research Foundation.

Johnson, C. W. 1985. *Bogs of the Northeast.* Hanover and London: University Press of New England.

Kiel, W. J. 1976. *Callophrys eryphon* (Lycaenidae) in Maine. *Jour. Lepid. Soc.* 30(1): 16–18.

Klots, A. B. 1951. *A Field Guide to the Butterflies of North America East of the Great Plains.* Boston: Houghton Mifflin Co.

_____. 1968. Boreal Sphagnum Bog Lepidoptera. *Bull. Assc. Minn Ent.* 2(4): 67.

Klots, A. B., and C. F. dos Passos. 1981. Studies of North American Erora (Scudder) (Lepidoptera, Lycaenidae). *Jour N. Y. Ent. Soc.* LXXXIX(4): 295–331.

Mikkola, K., and J. D. Lafontaine. 1994. Recent Introductions of Riparian Noctuid Moths from the Palearctic Region to North America. . . . *Jour. Lepid. Soc.,* 48(2):121–27.

Opler, P. A., and V. Malikul. 1992. *A Field Guide to Eastern Butterflies.* Boston, New York, London: Houghton Mifflin Co.

Platt, A. F. 1987. Banded Admirals from Western Maryland: Analysis of the Limenitis (Basilarchia) Arthemis-Astyanax Complex (Lepidoptera: Nymphalidae) at Green Ridge State Forest. *Proc. Ent. Soc. Wash.* 89(4): 633–45.

Scott, J. A. 1986. *The Butterflies of North America.* Stanford, Calif: Stanford University Press.

Stack, N. G., and A. W. Bell. 1995. *Field Guide to New England Alpine Summits.* Boston: Appalachian Mountain Club.

A Final Note

Times have changed since early naturalists amassed large collections of butterflies and other animals; threats to many individual species of plants and animals and to biodiversity are real and pressing. This is made all too clear in Appendix C. Therefore, unless you are able, as Warren Kiel is, to contribute scientific information to the study of butterflies, we exhort you to observe these beautiful creatures in their habitat and do not collect or in any way disturb them. You will find that the rewards for using your binoculars or camera instead of a net or a jar will still be great. Tips on observing butterflies in this way can be found in, among other books, R. M. Pyle's *The Audubon Society Field Guide to North American Butterflies* and Jeffrey Glassberg's *Butterflies through Binoculars: The East* (1999). You can also surround yourself with butterflies all season by planting a butterfly garden; there are now many books that can help you plan one that is appropriate for your region. A good place to start might be Opler and Mailikul's *A Field Guide to Eastern Butterflies,* which is listed in Recommended References.

Index

About the Author

Warren J. Kiel began studying butterflies, among other natural-history subjects, as a teenager. He is the generally acknowledged local expert on the lepidoptera of northern New Hampshire, especially the White Mountain region. This is his first book. He works as a skilled craftsman of fine furniture and lives in Whitefield, New Hampshire.

About the Artist

Lois De Luca is a graduate of Syracuse University School of Fine Arts. She studied drawing with Hans Hofmann, woodcuts with Antonio Frasconi, and etching with Stanley Hayter.

Lois has written and illustrated, with woodcuts, the children's book *How Big Am I?* Nature and nature drawing have been lifelong interests. She currently lives with her husband in Hancock, New York.